Equipping Christians for SPIRITUAL WARFARE

Charles Gordon, D.Th.

Detroit, MI, USA

Equipping Christians for Spiritual Warfare
Copyright © 2009, 2016 Charles Gordon, Sr.

All scripture quotations, unless otherwise indicated, are taken from the HOLY BIBLE, KING JAMES VERSION and are marked (KJV).

This work is the complete dissertation of Charles Gordon, Sr. submitted to Ashland Theological Seminary.

All rights reserved. No part of this publication may be reproduced, stored in a retrieval system, or transmitted in any form or by any means – electronic, mechanical, photocopy, recording, or any other – except for brief quotations in printed reviews, without the prior permission of the publisher.

*Priority*ONE Publications
P. O. Box 34722 • Detroit, MI 48234
E-mail: info@priorityonebooks.com
URL: http://www.priorityonebooks.com

ISBN 13:   978-1-933972-50-3
ISBN 10:   1-933972-50-5

Editing, Cover, and Interior design by PriorityONE Publications

Printed in the United States of America

ABSTRACT

The purpose of this project was to measure the impact of a six-week course at Unity Baptist Church in Detroit, Michigan on the participants' understanding of spiritual warfare, as well as the identification and use of God's armor. Pedagogical emphasis was on theology, biblical exegesis, spiritual conflict, and the Presence of God through the Holy Spirit. Measuring the impact of the course was found to be biblically sound and useful for the church.

CONTENTS

LIST OF TABLES vii

ACKNOWLEDGMENTS viii

Chapters

1. INTRODUCTION AND RATIONALE 9
2. BIBLICAL, THEOLOGICAL, AND HISTORICAL FOUNDATIONS 29
3. REVIEW OF THE LITERATURE 57
4. METHODOLOGY 85
5. PROJECT OUTCOMES 91
6. REFLECTIONS AND IMPLICATIONS 101

Appendix

1. PROPOSAL 113
2. SPIRITUAL WARFARE SURVEY 135
   Unity Baptist Church, Detroit, Michigan, Pre and Post-Test

WORKS CITED 137

REFERENCES 141

AUTHOR BIOGRAPHY 147

LIST OF TABLES

Table

1. Reported understanding spiritual warfare and the doctrine of Satan (Goals Two and Five)   94

2. Participants Learned the Concepts of the Full Armor (Weapons) of God   97

3. Participants deepened their awareness of the Holy Spirit's ministry in Christians against Satan and the forces of darkness   98

ACKNOWLEDGEMENTS

I give glory to my Lord and Savior Jesus Christ, for keeping me and for anointing me for this project.

To Dr. Deborah Dennis, a great advisor, and faithful servant of our Lord and Savior, Jesus Christ. You have helped me and never gave up on me. Thank you for being there for me. May God continue to bless you and your family.

To my Pastor, Dr. Valmon D. Stotts, Thanks for having faith in me during my setback and trying times. I also thank you for letting me complete the class project at your church, Unity Baptist Church, Detroit, Michigan. May God continue to bless you and your family. Thank you, Mrs. Stotts for your prayers and support.

There are many participants responsible for this document. God's wonderful people have allowed me the time to conduct the research needed for this study. I would like to offer a special thanks to the following individuals: Regina A. Dubose, Timothy Hyter, Rev. Jiles Burgines, Joy Bannister, Kelana Stewart, Timothy Peterson Jr., Dea. Reginald Harbin, Kevin Bannister, Rev. Robert Royal, and Deacon Willie and Mrs. Stokes.

Thanks to Mr. and Mrs. McNiel for their encouragement. A special thanks to Mrs. Janice McNiel for all her hard (word processing) work. She supported me through this project. May God continue to bless your family.

To Rev. and Mrs. Thomas Hamm, and to Rev. and Mrs. Edmund P. Morgan. Your encouragement, thoughtfulness, and sincerity will never be forgotten. Thanks for your support and prayers. God bless you.

To Pastor Kenneth James Flowers, my Father in the Ministry, who has provided me with wonderful support for many years. To Mrs. Kimberly Flowers, thanks for your support and words of encouragement. May God continue to bless you both and your family.

A special thanks to my wife, Rev. Sandra K. Gordon, who was a pillar of faith to me throughout this project. I love you. A true love blessed by God sent from above.

CHAPTER ONE

INTRODUCTION AND RATIONALE

Seek Christ and Christians for support
during times of Satan's attacks.

This was my interpretation of Eph. 6:11. The New International Version (NIV) will be used throughout this document unless otherwise noted. Christians battle against rulers and authorities, the powerful evil forces of fallen angels headed by Satan, a vicious fighter (1 Pet. 5:8). To withstand these attacks, believers must pray in the Spirit. They must depend on God's strength and use every piece of His armor.

The study of spiritual warfare was very interesting as I explored the various ideologies of the spiritual conflict. Sometimes, however, spiritual warfare can be overwhelming. It is important to understand the nature of spiritual warfare and the reality of human existence in order to be able to understand oneself as an individual and as a Christian. It is God's Spirit that gives believers the courage to take decisive action. The Holy Spirit reminds everyone to remain open to the truth because the final word is not cast from humanity. It belongs to God.

I discussed spiritual warfare with many Christians with a focus on the Kingdom of Light versus the Kingdom of Darkness. I was astonished at the extent of awareness of the Christians and their response to the Kingdom of Light and the Kingdom of Darkness. They were firm in their conviction that spiritual strength and courage are necessary for spiritual warfare and that they have no sufficient strength of their own. All sufficiency is derived from God.

PURPOSE STATEMENT

The purpose of this project was to measure the impact of a six-week course at Unity Baptist Church in Detroit, Michigan on the participants' understanding of spiritual warfare as well as the identification and use of God's armor. The research question was: What is the impact of a six-week course in equipping participants to understand spiritual warfare as well as to identify and effectively use God's armor?

OVERVIEW

The specific focus of this project was to help the participants understand the nature of spiritual warfare and thereby equip them for encountering forces of darkness. The aim of the project was to introduce scriptures that were particularly meaningful to the participants in training for spiritual warfare.

This project explored concepts like "spiritual warfare" and "equipping." To accomplish the purpose of the project, participants were encouraged to pray without ceasing. Participants shared in scripture reading, study time, prayer, and meditation through which they were able to experience God's wisdom and power. The group met at Unity Baptist Church for two hours each week for six weeks. During this time, participants increased in their understanding and knowledge of spiritual warfare. They learned the different types of prayer and weapons for spiritual warfare. The full armor (Eph. 6:14-18) is composed of "truth, righteousness, peace, faith, prayer, salvation, and the sword of the Spirit," which is the word of God.

Participants were guided in group interaction and personal reflection on Christ-like behavior, choices, and spirituality. One of the major truths presented in the class was that Satan wants control of our minds (Acts 14:2; 2 Cor. 4:4; 2 Cor. 11:3). This was clearly illustrated in scripture readings of Satan's attacks on biblical characters. His main tactics attempt to subvert the human mind. Satan attempts to deceive, to cause people to misunderstand and come to the wrong conclusions about truth. He wants believers to forget or veer from a focused spiritual path. Satan knows that if he can corrupt the mind, the individual will be unable to perceive the will of God.

RATIONALE

I contend Christians need divine help to deal with Satan's attacks. Any educational opportunity to equip Christians for spiritual warfare can benefit the church and help strengthen the individual believer. Too many

Christians are deceived, tricked, lured, and defeated by Satan. Satan is not God. However, he has a whole host of evil angels called demons that he can call upon for evil spiritual attacks. In order for Christians to effectively live freed from the bondage of sin and not be entangled in the snares of the devil, they must understand spiritual warfare.

A six-week course held at Unity Baptist Church, Detroit, Michigan focused on helping the participants understand spiritual warfare, as well as identifying and using the armor of God. The course provided insight on how Christians can be equipped for spiritual warfare. Moreover, there were personal, biblical, historical, theological, and contemporary perspectives that underscored the need for this course.

PERSONAL RATIONALE

It is out of my personal experience of spiritual warfare that I have a passion to equip followers of Jesus for spiritual warfare. The struggles and challenges with Satan have made me cry out to the Lord. The various satanic schemes against me such as loneliness, disappointment and discouragement are often understood as normal feelings, but left alone they are tools in the hands of Satan. It is out of these experiences that the Lord has chosen, called, anointed, and equipped me with a passion to help equip Christians for spiritual warfare.

My personal experience with the church informs me that many Christians underestimate the evil one's warfare against Christians. Consequently, our pews are filled with Christians who do not understand "spiritual warfare" and are not equipped to defeat Satan. For this reason, Christians are falling victim to Satan's attacks resulting in their feeling defeated, frustrated, and actually living in bondage to sin. There are many broken and wounded Christians who do not believe that actively engaging in spiritual warfare is a proactive approach to our faith. Moreover, many of the disciples in our churches are unlearned when it comes to the resources God has provided for us to use in encounters with the evil one.

Many believers shy away from any discussion about spiritual warfare. Discussions about Satan, demons, evil principalities, and power frighten a great number of Christians. To ignore this enemy and hope he will ignore us is both unrealistic and hazardous. I contend, Christians should put their faith and trust in God. With the help of the Holy Spirit, the devil's schemes can be overcome. Christians should put their faith and trust in God.

BIBLICAL RATIONALE

Spiritual warfare is presented in scripture as an integral part of the Godly life experience. The biblical research in both the Old and New Testament scriptures revealed several examples of the reality of spiritual warfare and the value and importance of God's armor in preparation for spiritual battle. In 1 Kings 18:16-30, the story of Elijah on Mount Carmel supports the reality of spiritual warfare and divine resources. The prophet Daniel and the three Hebrew boys also reveal that spiritual warfare is an integral part of the godly life experiences. The Bible reveals the loving nature of God (John 3:16) who provides for all Christians, armor that is available to all for protection against the wiles of the devil (Eph.6:10-18). Dr. Warren Wiersbe said, "Satan is a strong enemy, so Paul exhorts us to be strong. Paul knows that the flesh is weak (Mark 14:38) and that we can overcome only in Christ's power" (Wiersbe 1997, c1992, S. 553). The Apostle Paul said, "And my God will meet all your needs according to his glorious riches in Christ Jesus" (Phil. 4:19).

The Holy Spirit, the empowering agent in the believers' lives is presented throughout scripture. The biblical research supports equipping Christians for spiritual warfare. The scriptures also supported understanding spiritual warfare and identifying as well as using God's armor. Once we recognize we are in spiritual warfare and God has given us the resources we may ask how do we receive this strength to stand. We have the strength to stand when we realize that we are seated with Christ in the heavenlies far above all of Satan's principalities and powers (1:19-23), and that the very power of God is available to us through the indwelling Spirit (Wiersbe 1997, c1992, S. 553).

Thus, the biblical rationale for this project was founded on biblical truths about Satan and individuals, who experienced the temptations and hidden snares of the devil. The biblical portrait of Satan is that he is real and is seeking whom he can destroy. Scripture clearly confirms that Satan is the foe of every human being, starting with the disobedience of Adam and Eve. The name "Satan" actually means adversary or one who opposes. This project was significant because Christians must be prepared for spiritual warfare. Our preparation included the scriptures because God's Word defines the armor we need to help us stand victoriously against satanic attacks.

In the Old Testament scriptures, according to Genesis in the beginning, God created the heavens and the earth. God also created man in His own image (Gen. 1:1-27) and for His glory (Isa. 43:7). The Lord God said, "The man has now become like one of us, knowing good and evil" (Gen. 3:22). Although mankind was created to glorify God, He created free beings, able to do His will or refuse. He knew some would choose the wrong way of sin.

Genesis also records the first recorded instance of sin which took place in Heaven. The angel Lucifer became ambitious to be equal with God. For this sin of pride, he was cast out of heaven and became the one whom the Bible describes as the devil or Satan (Isa. 14: 12-14). Spiritual warfare exists first in heaven. Isa. 14:12 laments, "How you have fallen from heaven, O Morning Star, son of the Dawn! You have been cast down to the earth, you who once laid low the nations." This scripture was interpreted as a description of the fall of Satan. War between the forces of good and evil was underway, and this warfare was happening in heaven.

Spiritual warfare is also defined as the invisible confrontation between the forces of God and the forces of the devil, the kingdom of God versus the kingdom of darkness. Unlike earthly warfare, spiritual warfare involves fighting an invisible enemy. Sometimes this battle brings about circumstances that can hurt humans physically, emotionally, mentally, or spiritually (2 Kings 6:15-18).

In the New Testament scriptures, the gospel writers penned several examples of Jesus' encounters with the devil (Matt. 4:1-11; Luke 8:26-39). Jesus knew the world is full of adversarial spirits (Luke 11:14-26). His encounter with Satan in the garden (Matt.26:36-46; Mark 14:32-42; Luke 22:39-46) also confirms spiritual warfare in our lives. Jesus' encounter with spiritual warfare indicates that we also should take a stand against the devil's schemes. Jesus provided an example for all Christians to follow for victory in spiritual warfare. Jesus used the Word of God and stood in the power of God and the Holy Spirit. The same power, Holy Spirit power is available for us (Acts 1:8; Phil. 2:13; 4:13). With the help of the Holy Spirit, the devil's schemes can be overcome. "The Spirit makes Christians one 'in Christ' and empowers them, not only for the mission of the church, but also for the moral and ethical life appropriate to those who understand themselves to be people of the new age" (Achtemeier 1985, 401).

The Apostle Paul warned the New Testament church that we must identify as well as use God's armor to protect ourselves against the wiles of the devil (Eph. 6:10-18). Paul's letter to the church at Ephesus was the foundation scripture for this project. Christians must protect themselves with God's armor. His message was relevant then and is relevant now. Satan was real then and is real now. The sword of the Spirit is the Word of God, which is the armor of defense and weapon of offense. Therefore, our responsibility included also putting on the full armor of God so we, as Christians, may be able to stand victoriously.

THEOLOGICAL RATIONALE

Demons attack the mind to gain a foothold in the lives of people. Satan blinds the minds of the unsaved taking them away from the light of the Gospel (2 Cor. 4:3-4). To resist demon influence one must guard against what he reads and what sort of television he permits himself to view.... If he is not wary, demon influence may merge into demon obsession. If not curbed, demon invasion may ultimately eventuate. (Murphy 1996, 49)

My theological reflections reveal that this project was significant because God's goal for believers is to be equipped and empowered for spiritual warfare. The theological rationale was founded on some theological perspectives concerning spiritual warfare and the armor of God. Pedagogical emphasis was on theology, biblical exegesis, spiritual conflict, and the Presence of God evident in the work of the Holy Spirit. A major question asked by many was whether spiritual warfare exists today. Certainly! Satan is at war with every believer and seeks to disturb the lives of Christians so they do not live as true children of God. The moment we trusted and accepted the Lord Jesus Christ as our personal Savior, we learned that spiritual warfare became a part of our life's struggle.

The doctrine of spiritual warfare was a prominent theme throughout this project. Spiritual warfare is the invisible confrontation between the forces of God and the forces of the devil, and the kingdom of God versus the kingdom of darkness. Edward Murphy, author of *The Handbook for Spiritual Warfare,* is of the opinion that spiritual warfare is the most perplexing problem ever challenged by the church/humanity (Murphy 1996, 17).

Harvey Cox, theologian from Harvard University, is against the use of the term *spiritual warfare.* He observed that,

> When we talk about spiritual warfare, however, we are not envisioning armed conflict or the provocation of hostilities among people. We are taking the adjective spiritual quite seriously. We are suggesting that life is not just biology; there is a uniquely spiritual dimension to reality. There are unseen personal forces that have an impact on day-to-day life. Not all of these spirits are positive and benevolent either. There are many that are evil and bent on destruction. The Bible calls Christians to be aware of this and to prepare for a struggle. The biblical metaphor of spiritual warfare, then, is a shorthand way of referring to our conflict with these spirit forces. They are perpetrators of untold evil in both the physical realm and the moral realm. The Bible describes these spirits as especially working to keep people from responding to the redemptive message of the Lord Jesus Christ and to bring about the demise of the people of God. The gospel of deliverance we bring to people is actually a message of peace and reconciliation. (Arnold 2003, 25)

Today, the study of spiritual warfare is too frightening for many Christians. However, to ignore this enemy and hope he will quietly go away is both unrealistic and hazardous. In his book, *Born for Battle,*

Arthur Mathews tells the reader:

> The terrifying face of a hostile world of evil and malicious spirit paralyzes many Christians into inactivity and unwillingness to seek out biblical answers and to apply them. There are many clear indications of Satan's motives and methods given to us in the Bible, if only we would heed them. His central purpose is to pull God from His throne in the minds of humans and to take that throne himself. (Mathews 1992, 127)

Whether we use the term "spiritual warfare" or not, my research substantiates the truth, Satan is real and the Christian is in a battle between the kingdom of light and the kingdom of darkness. The devil is still active, roaming in the shadows, looking for vulnerable prey. He does not stop his activity and neither can we. Christians must not stop or avoid the tasks appointed by God, but claim the protection God offers from the enemy's forces.

Understanding the doctrine of Satan was also a prominent theme in this project. In order for the Christian to be prepared for spiritual warfare, my research suggested the importance of understanding the enemy. My study revealed that the classic position of the Christian Church was that Satan and demons are spiritual entities that exist and sometimes manifest their presence in the world (Arnold 2003, 49). The primary focus of these entities was and is the spiritual deception of humanity. Their primary mission is to thwart God's purposes on earth and specifically prevent non-believers from placing their faith in Christ Jesus and prevent Christians from being effective disciples of Jesus (Wardle 2004, 2).

The doctrine of the Holy Spirit was a prominent theme throughout this project. The presence of God within the believer inspires and empowers us with qualities we would not otherwise possess. Satan desires that which is wrong, corrupt, and perverse. God's Spirit gives believers the courage to take decisive action and empowers us for victorious living.

The Holy Spirit is important to the process of spiritual warfare and change. The Scriptures reveal the Holy Spirit is one who comforts, rebukes, corrects, and trains Christians in righteousness. It is therefore essential to be thoroughly equipped with the Scriptures and the Holy Spirit to be prepared for every good work. Paul shows what it means to be in a Holy Spirit environment when he states:

> Eyes have not seen and ears have not heard, no mind has conceived what God has prepared for those who love Him- but God has revealed it to us by His Spirit. The Spirit searches all things, even the deep things of God. For who among men knows the thoughts of a man except the man's spirit with-in him? In the same way no one knows the thoughts of God except the Spirit who is from God, that we may understand what God has freely given us. This is what we speak, not in words taught by human wisdom but in words taught by the Spirit, expressing spiritual truths in spiritual words. (1 Cor. 2:9-13)

The better equipped we are for spiritual warfare, the more effective we will be in our spiritual journey. However, we must remember God is the only one who is all powerful; Satan is not. Whenever Satan perpetrates evil against the children of God, God uses that evil to accomplish His will. God can also turn into good what Satan means for evil. Through Jesus Christ we can stand triumphant in spiritual conflict. We know God lives in the believer and the believer lives in God. Thus we know and rely on the love God has for His children. With faith in God and identifying and using God's armor, we are equipped to become more than conquerors against spiritual warfare.

The Christian's warfare (conflict) is preeminently a spiritual warfare for which all the armor necessary to obtain victory has been provided (Eph. 6:10-20). It follows that Christians should practice spiritual discipline and possesses an unwavering faith in God. The critical battle was won at Calvary. Therefore, the emphasis in a passage like Ephesians 6:10-20 is not so much on the gaining of new ground but on the holding of what has already been won.

> We, as Christians, live behind enemy lines and whether we like it or not, are involved in the war in two ways. As those attacked by Satan, we ourselves are a battlefield.

> And as those commissioned to join with Jesus in taking territory from Satan, we are soldiers in Jesus' army. (Kraft and White 2000, 20)

My research and experience with spiritual warfare has affirmed that we must depend on the power of God and the Holy Spirit for guidance. The spiritual armor provides a defense in matters of the flesh, the world, and the devil. When we embrace righteousness, faith, salvation, prayer, the sword of the Spirit, and the Word of God, we will stand more than conquerors against the demonic.

HISTORICAL RATIONALE

The purpose of this project was to measure the impact of a six-week course at Unity Baptist Church in Detroit, Michigan on the participants' understanding of spiritual warfare as well as their identification of and use of God's armor. All of human history and all human divine encounters have taken place in the context of spiritual warfare. The entire biblical account, from Genesis to the Revelation, and the Church has discovered and concluded that spiritual warfare exists in the universe. Edward Murphy in his book *The Handbook for Spiritual Warfare* said, "At some point in the hidden past rebellion occurred within the angelic kingdom, the Kingdom of God and the Kingdom of Satan" (Murphy 1996, 13).

Philosopher Lactantius who lived, between 260-340 A.D., quoted a statement believed to be written by Greek philosopher Epicurus between 341-270 B.C.:

> God either wishes to take away evils and is unable; or he is able and unwilling; or he is neither willing nor able, or he is both willing and able. If he is willing and is unable, he is feeble, which is not in accordance with the character of God; if he is able and unwilling, he is envious, which is equally at variance with God; if he is neither willing nor able, he is both envious and feeble, and therefore not God; if he is both willing and able, which alone is suitable to God, from what source then are evils? Or why does he not remove them? (Murphy 1996, 17)

Gregory Boyd, author of *God at War: The Bible and Spiritual Conflict,* concurs with other great historians who have found references to spiritual warfare throughout the ages. Gregory Boyd states:

> The figure Satan continues to permeate the thinking of the Church in other respects throughout history, at least up until the time of the Enlightenment. As was said, the Church retained at least an echo of the warfare worldview. But in terms of arriving at an ultimate explanation for evil, after Augustine, the question always gets filed under the category of God's providence instead of under the category of spiritual warfare, that is, under the topic of what Satan, rebel angels, and fallen humans freely choose to do against God's will. With Augustine, it becomes a problem of understanding evil as part of God's will (Boyd 1997, 55).

Spiritual warfare is an integral part of the entire Christian experience. The hosts of Satan are committed to hinder and obstruct the work of Christ. It is a fact of life. Satan desires that which is wrong, corrupt, and perverse. Our goals, as believers, should be to gain an accurate and sober-minded understanding of spiritual warfare. Our goal also should be not to be led astray by a tainted view originating from frightening superstitions and odd practices.

Although Satan is a strong enemy, we know God will stand with us and fight against the schemes of the devil. God's righteousness can be worn as our breastplate to protect us from Satan's temptations. In the midst of the struggle between right and wrong, we can trust God to make available the resources we need to experience against Satan. Historians remind us that spiritual warfare is a lifelong spiritual battle and we must understand it and effectively use the armor God has provided.

CONTEMPORARY RATIONALE

The Christian church within the past decade recognizes more than ever the need for Christians to be equipped for spiritual warfare. Moreover, the church acknowledges that Christians must understand spiritual warfare. It is imperative that we identify as well as use the armor of God as our weapon of defense.

Contemporary writers of this century, such as Charles Hodges, Joyce Meyers, Charles Stanley, Neil T. Anderson, Elizabeth Alves, and Augustus Strong, have one key thing in common. They argue that many Christians behave as though their personal strength in spiritual warfare is limited. I have learned that we must depend on the authority, strength, wisdom, and discernment of Jesus Christ.

Although Christians, like the Apostle Paul, are merely weak human beings, God's plans and methods can be used to win battles against Satan. The Apostle Paul supports this conclusion. He said in Eph. 6:10-18,

> Finally, be strong in the Lord and in his mighty power. Put on the full armor of God so that you can take your stand against the devil's schemes. For our struggle is not against flesh and blood, but against the rulers, against the authorities, against the powers of this dark world and against the spiritual forces of evil in the heavenly realms. Therefore, put on the full armor of God, so that when the day of evil comes, you may be able to stand your ground, and after you have done everything, to stand. Stand firm then, with the belt of truth buckled around your waist, with the breastplate of righteousness in place and with your feet fitted with the readiness that comes from the gospel of peace. In addition to all this, take up the shield of faith, with which you can extinguish all the flaming arrows of the evil one. Take the helmet of salvation and the sword of the Spirit, which is the word of God. And pray in the Spirit on all occasions with all kinds of prayers and requests. With this in mind, be alert and always keep on praying for all the saints.

To further support the reality that God's plans and methods can be used to defeat Satan. Paul said in 2 Cor. 10: 3-5,

> For though we live in the world, we do not wage war as the world does. The weapons we fight with are not the weapons of the world. On the contrary, they have divine power to demolish strongholds. We demolish arguments and every pretension that sets itself up against the knowledge of God, and we take captive every thought to make it obedient to Christ.

"Christians must learn the important area of spiritual warfare and how to distinguish spiritual power that comes from God, and spiritual power that is from the enemy" (Kraft 2002, 11). Chuck Lawless wrote the article, "But who are you? Churches that threaten the enemy" to remind us that, "The enemy will do everything he can to keep nonbelievers in their darkness, and only God is powerful enough to overcome that darkness" (Betts 2006, 4).

Believers of Christ must oppose the spirits of darkness that blind and deceive the minds of the heavens. Charles Kraft and Mark White state:

> One of Satan's primary tactics to thwart God's plans is to get God's people to disobey him or to neglect their relationship with him. This the enemy does most effectively through either keeping people ignorant of what God desires (2 Corinthians 4:4) or by deceiving them into disobeying (Genesis 3:1-7). (Kraft and White 2000, 47)

Evil forces that have hindered efforts to reach people with the Gospel must be resisted. "Our goal is to see men and women-believers and unbelievers-set free from the bondage of Satan by the power of the blood of Jesus. Satan is merely a created being, while God is "the great uncreated Creator" (Murphy 1996, 27).

I have also gained a deeper understanding and appreciation for praise. I learned praise is really an assault weapon against Satan. When Joshua and the children of Israel faced the Jericho wall they praised their way through to victory.

> Joshua got up early the next morning and the priests took up the ark of the LORD. The seven priests carrying the seven trumpets went forward, marching before the ark of the LORD and blowing the trumpets. The armed men went ahead of them and the rear guard followed the ark of the LORD, while the trumpets kept sounding. So on the second day they marched around the city once and returned to the camp. They did this for six days. On the seventh day, they got up at daybreak and marched around the city seven times

in the same manner, except that on that day they circled the city seven times. The seventh time around, when the priests sounded the trumpet blast, Joshua commanded the people, "Shout! For the LORD has given you the city! The city and all that is in it are to be devoted to the LORD. (JOS. 6:12-17A)

When spiritual conflict comes, praise the Lord, not for the evil but as a declaration of war against it. "Therefore, if anyone is in Christ, he/she is a new creation. The old has gone; the new has come" (2 Cor. 5:17). Still, some Christians hesitate, believing that "postmodernity is the bane of Christian faith, the new enemy taking over the role of secular humanism as object of fear and primary target of demonization" (Smith 2006, 18).

I agree with Charles Kraft who argues, "For we, as Christians, have much to learn in this important area, including how to distinguish spiritual power that is from God, and spiritual power that is from the enemy" (Kraft 2002, 11). We must believe that strength and victory can be found only through an unwavering faith in God and using the resources God has provided.

CONTEXT

The purpose of this project was to measure the impact of a six-week course at Unity Baptist Church in Detroit, Michigan on the participants' understanding of spiritual warfare as well as the identification and use of God's armor.

The Unity Baptist Church, located in Detroit, Michigan, was chosen as the location of the project. From the very beginning, Unity Baptist Church has been committed to the mandate of making disciples for Christ. The Unity has emphatically sought to serve the Lord, its people, and the community. Equipping the people of God for life, service, and encounters with spiritual warfare has continued to be a major focus of its Pastor and people.

On March 17, 1963, Reverend Valmon D. Stotts was called to the pastorate of Unity Baptist Church. Reverend Stotts, pastor and visionary took seriously his responsibility as pastor to preach and teach the

Scriptures. Moreover, according to scripture he was chosen to perfect, equip, and build up the body of Christ so that the church would experience unity and maturity in Christ (Eph. 4: 11-12). Pastor Stotts established a Christian education program that was designed to enhance the spiritual knowledge and growth of the entire church. Through preaching, teaching, and caring, the Pastor and staff have equipped its people with God's resources for all areas in life.

The Pastor's emphasis on Christian growth also included anyone or anything that hindered spiritual growth. Scripture reveals that Satan, our enemy, is a roaring lion seeking to devour God's people (1Pet. 5:8). Therefore, the church must equip Christians for spiritual warfare. Our encounter in spiritual warfare made this project significant for the Unity Church.

In support of my Pastor's vision to equip the church through God's Word, made the Unity Church an excellent location to house the first course. I was not surprised when Pastor Stotts agreed to host the six-week course on spiritual warfare. Neither was I amazed by the willingness of the Unity Church members to participate in this project. The project requirements did not mandate membership in the Unity Church or a specific age, race, or educational background. The participants were only required to attend all classes and open to receive instruction.

The participants in the course were adult middle-class African Americans. Three of the participants were preachers; two participants serve in the church as one of the church soloist and the other a deacon. The participants also included a Michigan Police officer. Four of the nine participants graduated from college; four participants are attending college; and the ninth participant recently graduated from high school.

The participants were hungry for more of God and His Word. They were also committed to spiritual growth. They positioned themselves and learned to identify as well as use the armor of God. With the anointing of the Holy Spirit and the armor of God, the Unity Baptist church disciples were equipped for spiritual warfare and are empowered to stand.

PROJECT GOALS

The purpose of this project was to measure the impact of a six-week course at Unity Baptist Church in Detroit, Michigan on the participants' understanding of spiritual warfare as well as the identification and use of God's armor. At the conclusion of the project, the following outcomes were anticipated for participants:

1. Learn the concepts of the full armor (weapons) of God.

2. Gain an awareness of Satan's attacks in their lives.

3. Demonstrate personal commitment to study the Biblical views of spiritual warfare.

4. Deepen their awareness of the work of the Holy Spirit in their personal lives.

5. Increase knowledge of spiritual warfare and grow in their ability to identify as well as equip themselves with the armor of God.

6. Encourage and able to "put on" the full armor of God and trust the Holy Spirit to empower them against the forces of darkness.

METHODOLOGY

The project aimed to equip members of the Unity Baptist Church for spiritual warfare. The research question was: What is the impact of a six-week course in equipping participants to understand spiritual warfare as well as to identify and effectively use God's armor?

The goals for the participants in this project were as follows: 1) they will understand spiritual warfare; 2) they will recognize Satan's attack in their lives; 3) they will identify the components of God's armor; 4) they will be equipped for spiritual warfare, and; 5) they will rely and trust the Holy Spirit to empower them against the forces of darkness.

The design of this project included lecturing, experiential learning and group process in leading participants in the understanding of spiritual warfare. The format of this project also included evaluating the impact of the six-week class in their lives. The project proceeded along the following course:

1. Requested approval from my pastor to offer the course at the Unity Baptist Church.

2. Scheduled dates and times for class sessions.

3. An open invitation was extended to members of Unity Baptist Church to participate in a six-week course.

4. Created a pre-and post-test survey with twelve statements pertaining to each member's knowledge of spiritual warfare and ability to identify as well as previously used the armor of God.

5. Determined the content and material that was taught to a group of Christians and the format in which the material was presented. After a review of literature and meditation, a determination was made regarding the content and material to be taught to a group of Christians that would encourage these individuals to develop a more intimate relationship with God. Pedagogical emphasis was on theology, biblical exegesis, spiritual conflict, and the Presence of God evident in the work of the Holy Spirit.

6. Prayed for the nine participants and the successfulness of the project and course.

7. Administered pre-test survey and distributed course syllabus at the first class and to the participants the first day of the six-week experience. The participants met for two hours each week for six weeks at the church.

8. Taught the prepared material and encouraged the participants to put into practice what they learned about using the full armor of God as their weapon against Satan.

9. Administered the post-test survey to measure the impact of the six-week group experience on each participant.

The outcome was measured by a pre-and post-survey that determined the impact of the six-week course. The pre-and post-test survey results determined the degree to which participants were equipped in their understanding of spiritual warfare and their ability to identify and effectively use God's armor.

PERSONAL GOALS

The Bible is my safeguard against false teaching, and God's grace gives me courage to take decisive action on spiritual matters. Because of the course on spiritual warfare and the understanding of God's armor, I am now better prepared to equip other Christians for spiritual warfare.

When God called me to begin this project, questions immediately arose. What is involved in helping others understand spiritual warfare? How can I prepare myself to effectively teach others? Spiritual warfare became a matter of prime importance to me. My life focused on seeking greater understanding to gain clarity for myself. Daily meditation and prayer were an integral part of my preparation. Scripture and academic readings were also vital to the success of this project. This project was a special gift from God to enable me to identify available resources for Christians. It is my mission to share with all believers what I have learned about spiritual warfare. My personal goals for the project were:

1. To increase my personal awareness of spiritual warfare and its impact on my daily life.

2. To be better prepared to equip Christians for spiritual warfare.

3. To experience personal growth from developing and implementing this project.

4. That I may gain a deeper personal intimate relationship with God through Jesus Christ and the Holy Spirit.

Plan of the Paper

The plan of this project was that a select group of participants from the Unity Baptist Church Detroit, Michigan would be equipped for spiritual warfare. The purpose of this project was to enhance their understanding of spiritual warfare and help them to identify as well as use the armor of God in their faith walk.

This chapter presented the structure and framework for this project. The context for understanding the relevancy of this project, the details of the design, the scope of the project, as well as the goals for achievement were also established in this chapter. The following chapters will include biblical, theological and historical foundations (Chapter Two); a review of contemporary literature (Chapter Three); a detailed description of the method, procedures, and design of the project (Chapter Four); and, project outcomes (Chapter Five). A final chapter will reflect on the findings as it applies to equipping Christians for spiritual warfare.

CHAPTER TWO

BIBLICAL, THEOLOGICAL AND HISTORICAL FOUNDATIONS

A mighty fortress is our God, A bulwark never failing
Our helper He amid the flood of mortal ills prevailing
For still our ancient foe doth seek to work us woe;
His craft and power are great and armed with cruel hate,
On earth is not is equal.

Did we in our own strength confide, our striving would be losing;
Were not the right Man on our side,
the Man of God's own choosing.
Dost ask who that may be?
Christ Jesus it is He; Lord Sabaoth His Name,
From age to age the same and he must win the battle.

And tho this world, with devils filled, should threaten to undo us,
We will not fear, for God hath willed His truth to triumph thru us.
The prince of darkness grim
We tremble not for him; His rage we can endure,
For lo! His doom is sure our little word shall fell him.

That word above the earthly powers no thanks to them abideth
The Spirit and the gifts are ours thru Him who with us sideth
Let goods and kindred go, this mortal life also;
[literally from the German:
"Let them take body, possessions, fame, child, and wife"]
The body they may kill: God's truth abideth still,
His kingdom is forever.

Written by Martin Luther

The aforementioned hymn aptly captures the thesis of this project to equip Christians for spiritual warfare. The purpose of this project is to measure the impact of a six-week course at Unity Baptist Church in Detroit, Michigan on the participants' understanding of spiritual warfare as well as their identification of and use of God's armor.

Spiritual warfare means different things to different people. The term itself is not found in the scriptures; however, the Bible does confirm that Christians are in a war. The Apostle Paul addresses the reality of Satan and spiritual warfare in his letters to the Ephesians and Corinthian churches (Eph. 6:10-12; 2 Cor. 10:3-5). A careful study of Paul's letters to the church informs us that our warfare is not with human beings but with the devil and his demons. Spiritual warfare is conflict originating in the invisible, spiritual realm that is also evident in the visible, physical realm. It refers both to the believer's multidimensional war against personal sin and the warfare with Satan and his fallen angels. Satan is a strong enemy. He attempts to defeat us with an array of evil strategies and through well-laid plans and deliberate deception. According to Dr. Edward Murphy, [author of his works] spiritual warfare is the most perplexing problem ever faced by humanity (Murphy 1996, 17).

Spiritual warfare is a proactive approach to faith in God. Christians actively pursue spiritual disciplines to become stronger and better prepared to resist the devil when faced with harassment by his demonic hosts. When in the position of spiritual bondage, Christians actively engage the enemy. Prayer is utilized as a weapon to penetrate strongholds that cannot be reached in any other way. Spiritual warfare is characterized by putting aside a passive attitude towards faith, release the pursuit of that which is of sole benefit and make a firm faith commitment to God. One should not seek a personal agenda, but instead submit to God's will and accept His desires. In order to be able to understand the strategies of Satan and the resources God has provided, we must study the scriptures, its history and traditions and walk by faith. This chapter presents the biblical, theological, and historical foundations that helped to form this project.

BIBLICAL FOUNDATION

Finally, be strong in the Lord and in his mighty power. Put on the full armor of God so that you can take your stand against the devil's schemes. For our struggle is not against flesh and blood, but against the rulers, against the authorities, against the powers of this dark world and against the spiritual forces of evil in the heavenly realms. Therefore, put on the full armor of God, so that when the day of evil comes, you may be able to stand your ground, and after you have done everything, to stand. (Eph. 6:10-13)

The scriptures tell me this project is important because spiritual warfare is an integral part of the entire Christian experience. Sometimes, however, understanding spiritual warfare can be mind-boggling and to some believers frightening. Thus, it is important to understand the nature of spiritual warfare and the reality of our need for God's armor to stand against the forces of darkness. To establish a biblical foundation for this project the following questions will be addressed: Is the devil real? Does the devil really exist? Who is Satan and where did he come from? Are demons real? What is the devil's mission? Is the church under satanic attack? If so, how does one resist the devil? What was Jesus' method of resisting Satan? What is sin and where did it begin? What do we mean by spiritual warfare? Is the church equipped for spiritual warfare? What are the resources God has provided to equip the church for spiritual warfare?

What is sin and where did it begin?

The biblical foundation begins with the initial creations of God and the subsequent sin in heaven. The angel Lucifer became ambitious and sought to become equal with God. For this sin of pride, he was cast out of heaven and became the one whom the Bible describes as the devil or Satan. No other angel in Heaven would have been closer to God and no other angel excelled Him in power. Ezekiel 28:17 discloses how Lucifer became enamored with himself and so focused on his beauty that he actually believed he deserved to be God. His proud attributes clouded his judgment. A war between the forces of good and evil was under way, and this warfare was happening in heaven. Isaiah 14:12 laments, "How you have fallen from heaven, O Morning Star, son of the dawn! You have been cast down to the earth, you who once laid low the nations." This scripture is interpreted as a description of the fall of Satan. For this sin of pride, Lucifer was cast out of heaven and became the one whom the Bible describes as the devil or Satan.

Old Testament scripture reveals the first recorded instance of sin took place in the Garden of Eden. In the beginning, God created heaven and earth. God also created man in His own image (Gen. 1:1-27) and for

His glory (Isa. 43:7). "The Lord God said, 'The man has now become like one of us, knowing good and evil" (Gen.3:22). Although mankind was created to glorify Him, God created free beings that were able to accept or refuse to do His will. He knew some would choose the wrong way of sin. Adam and Eve sought to please themselves at the cost of displeasing God (Gen. 3:1-6). According to Harper's Bible Dictionary,

> This idea lies at the heart of the Genesis account of the beginning of sin (Gen. 3:1-7), where the essential problem lies in the desire of the humans to 'be like God.' All sin is an act of idolatry, the attempt to replace the Creator with someone or something else; usually one's own self or one's own creation. Paul understood this very well, as he indicates in Rom. 1:18-3:20: all humankind lies under condemnation because all are idolaters of one type or another. (Achtemeier 1985, 955)

Sin is, according to D.R.W. Wood, the *New Bible Dictionary*, a violation of that which God's glory demands and is, therefore, in its essence the contradiction of God (New Bible Dictionary, 1996).

Who is Satan and what does he really want?

Satan was originally created as an anointed cherub. A cherub was not only an angel, but an angel that guarded the throne of God. The Bible does not state when the creation of angels took place yet, scriptures reveal they already existed when God created the world. Scriptures also clearly confirm that Satan is the foe of every human being, starting with Adam and Eve. Satan is an enemy of the humanity. Satan's name means adversary and his name characterizes his mission to oppose, to resist, and to hinder the purpose and plan of God (Rev.12:7-9).

Satan attacks are personal, often involving our hearts, emotions, and faith. Satan means "adversary," because he is the enemy of God. Charles Ryrie describes Satan as an antagonist of God and His people. The very name Satan means adversary (1 Pet. 5:8), while the word devil means slanderer (Rev 12:10) (Ryrie 1985). In the Anchor Bible, Ryrie defines his name as accuser, adversary or slanderer (Ryrie 1995). He is also called the tempter (Matt. 4:3), and the murderer and the liar (John 8:44). Devil means "accuser," because he accuses God's people day and night before the throne of God (Rev. 12:7-11).

M. G. Easton in the Easton Bible Dictionary pens this description of Satan.

> He is "the constant enemy of God, of Christ, of the divine kingdom, of the followers of Christ, and of all truth; full of falsehood and all malice, and exciting and seducing to evil in every possible way." His power is very great in the world. He is a "roaring lion, seeking whom he may devour" (1 Pet. 5:8). Men are said to be "taken captive by him" (2 Tim. 2:26). Christians are warned against his "devices" (2 Cor. 2:11), and called on to "resist" him (James 4:7). Christ redeems his people from "him that had the power of death, that is, the devil" (Heb. 2:14). Satan has the "power of death," not as lord, but simply as executioner. (Easton 1996)

Paul Achtemeier in the Harper's Bible Dictionary gives us a glimpse of what Satan really wants. He explains that,

> Satan and his cohorts then came to represent the powers of evil in the universe and were even known in Jesus' time as the Kingdom of Satan, against which Jesus had come to fight and to establish the Kingdom of God (e.g., Mark 3:23-26). The demons were considered to be the cause of sickness, both physical and mental, and of many calamities of nature (e.g., storms, earthquakes); in general, they were the forces responsible for much of human sin (and therefore misery), and they were always opposed to God's purposes and God's people. (Achtemeier 1985, 909)

We must beware of the wiles of the devil (Eph. 6:11) which means his strategy, devices (2 Cor. 2:11) and snares (1 Tim. 3:7). He is the ruler of darkness and uses darkness (ignorance and lies) to further his plans (2 Cor. 4:1; Luke 22:53).

> Satan wants to capture our minds because he knows the mind is the leader of all actions. He knows the value in capturing our minds since our actions are a direct result of our thoughts (Acts 14:2; 2 Cor. 4: 4; 11:3). When Satan attacked biblical characters, his main tactic was to subvert their minds. Satan's battle strategy is simple. His strategic plans were designed to deceive God's people and cause them to forget or misunderstand His truth (Kraft and White 2000, 47).

As the father of all lies he endeavored to lead Christians to the wrong conclusions about truth or redirect their focus (John 8:44). Satan is out to deceive us, to trick us into buying his lies and temptations.

Satan is limited, he is not present everywhere, he is not all-knowing, and he is not all-powerful. Satan has a whole host of evil angels called demons that he can call upon for spiritual evil attacks, but he is not God. Once Satan has established a strong foothold in a person's life (Eph. 4:27), he will often unmask himself to torment and enslave his victim further. Although limited in his knowledge, Satan understands that a corrupted mind will be unable to perceive the will of God. Satan wants the Christian life to be lived in bondage to sin.

> The people of God are in a spiritual battle with Satan. There is a spiritual war going on and that spiritual war in the unseen world is driving events in our own visible world. There is no peace in the material world because there is a war now raging in the spiritual world. Why is it that, for all our professed ideals, our hopes, and our skills, peace on earth is still a distant objective seen only dimly through the storms and turmoil of our present difficulties? (Stedman 2007, 10)

What are demons and what do they do?

According to William Evans, the origin of demons is not revealed in the Bible. However, they are thought to be angels who fell with Satan

(Matt. 25:41; Rev. 12:7, 9). Similar to Satan, demons attempt to thwart the purpose of God in every way possible (Dan 10:10-14; Rev 16:13-16).

Our lusts and desires leave us wide open to attacks and influences of Satan and his demons. Unless we know who the enemy is, where he is, and what he can do, we have a difficult time defeating him. Satan is a strong enemy. He does not engage us in open warfare, but deals in wiles and strategies, of which we need to watch against and be prepared. Christians were warned that Satan fights with lies that may sound very much like the truth. We must to arm ourselves with God's truth in order to defeat Satan's lies. The strategies of Satan confirm the Christians understanding of Satan and spiritual warfare.

What do we mean by spiritual warfare?
Is the church equipped for spiritual warfare?

Both the Old and New Testament scriptures reveal several examples of the reality of spiritual warfare and the value and importance of God's armor in preparation for battle. In the Old Testament scripture, we discover Adam's sin consisted in his yielding to the assaults of temptation and eating the forbidden fruit. Yes, spiritual warfare. According to the *Easton Bible Dictionary,* Adam's sin involved in it, the sin of unbelief, virtually making God a liar; and the guilt of disobedience to God's command. He fell short of the glory of God, lost the favor of God and communion with Him. Adam's whole nature became depraved, and he and humanity incurred the penalty of sin (Easton Bible Dictionary, 1996).

In the New Testament, the gospel writers penned several examples of Jesus' encounter with the devil. Jesus knew the world is full of enemy spirits and that they are very successful at victimizing people. Jesus Himself was tested by Satan in the wilderness after He has fasted 40 days and nights (Matt. 4:1-11). Whenever Jesus was confronted with people filled with demons, in faith, He cast out the demons (Matt. 8:28-34). Even when Jesus was in the garden of Gethsemane, Satan sought to obstruct the plan of God for our salvation (Mark 14:32-41). Jesus' encounter with spiritual warfare models what we should do to take our stand against the devil's schemes.

The Apostle Paul wrote in the New Testament that as Christians we must identify and use God's armor to protect ourselves from the wiles of the devil. The book of Ephesians, written to the church in Ephesus is a letter of encouragement. Paul describes the nature and appearance of the Church, and admonishes believers to function as the living body of Christ on earth. Paul warns the church of its battle against Satan and the powers of this dark world. He also informs the Christians of the threat we face against a powerful army whose goal is to defeat Christ's Church.

Evil spiritual forces constantly are encouraging undesirable tendencies within Christians, such as pride, lust, envy, anger, lying, and rage. Spence-Jones concluded in The Pulpit Commentary: Ephesians that

> To be strong is our duty; to be weak is our sin. Strong trust, strong courage, strong endurance, strong hope, strong love, may all be had from him, if only our fellowship with him be maintained in uninterrupted vigor. Our chief enemy does not engage us in open warfare, but deals in wiles and stratagems, which need to be watched against and prepared for with peculiar care (Spence-Jones 2004, 258).

Satan attempts to influence spiritual minds to mimic these behaviors.

> So I find this law at work: When I want to do good, evil is right there with me. For in my inner [spirit] being I delight in God's law; but I see another law at work in the members of my body, waging war against the law of my [spirit] mind and making me a prisoner of the law of sin at work within my members.

Although we are assured of victory, we must engage in the struggle until Christ returns. Since the battle is not of earthly origin, we need divine help to deal with the devil's attacks.

What are the resources God has provided to equip the church for spiritual warfare?

The biblical foundation would be incomplete without researching what the New Testament scriptures teach about the armor God provides for our victory against Satan. We can overcome the devil's schemes with the help of the Holy Spirit. The Holy Spirit speaks to the inner being and provides guidance as to the right things to do. When we listen and follow this spiritual path, we will remain under the control and protection of the Holy Spirit. When we remain vigilant in asking through prayer for God's spirit to lead and guide us, we will be prepared and equipped for spiritual warfare. Ephesians 6:17-18 affirms that the sword of the Spirit is the Word of God, which is our armor of defense and weapon of offense. Our responsibility includes putting our faith and trust in God. Our responsibility also includes putting on the full armor of God so we, as Christians, may be able to stand victoriously (Eph. 6:11-13). What are some of the other weapons recommended in scripture to combat satanic attacks?

First, in the war against Satan, James the brother of Jesus encourages the believer to draw near to God. "Submit yourselves therefore to God. Resist the devil, and he will flee from you. Draw near to God and he will draw near to you" (James 4:7-8). As we move closer to God, He requires us to surrender to Him, seek His ways and maintain a sincere resolution to turn away from evil influences. The rewards of being in His presence include Satan taking flight. God is relational and has always desired fellowship with us. Our relationship with Christ will strengthen our efforts against satanic attack.

Second, in the war against Satan, the scripture supports the discipline of prayer as a weapon for Christians to combat satanic attack. In Luke 18:1, Jesus taught His disciples to always pray and to never lose heart. God created prayer as a means of communication between Himself and His people. Prayer is the vehicle by which to commune with the invisible God. It is the medium through which the spirit is intended to affect and be affected by the will and purpose of the divine creator. All Christian endeavors, including prayer, should be born out of our desire for intimacy with God. Apostle Paul said to the Corinthians, "I am afraid that just as Eve was deceived by the serpent's cunning, your minds may somehow be led astray from your sincere and pure devotion to Christ" (2 Cor. 11:13).

Prayer is a powerful tool against Satan. As redeemed believers, we must realize, there is power in prayer. Jesus told Peter that Satan desired to sift him, but He prayed his faith would not fail them (Luke 22:31). Jesus tells how Satan had sought to have the disciples in order to sift them and lead them to fall away from Jesus. Jesus prayed for Peter so that he would not fail in his faith and thus be able to strengthen the others. In John 17:15, Jesus prayed that we would be kept from the evil one. When we draw near to God in prayer and He draws near to us, we will experience the power of prayer in our combat with the satanic.

Lastly, in the war against Satan warfare of praise has also been one of the mightiest weapons that God has given to His people. We find in Psalm 149:8 one of the greatest scriptures on how praise can hinder the devil's schemes.

> The high praises of God are to be in the mouths of the Lord's people. Such praises have magnificent results. They are like a two-edged sword in the hands of the saints. They bring vengeance and punishment upon the ungodly. They bind their kings with chains, and their nobles with fetters of iron. (Life Application Study Bible 1997, 1272)

Christian praise would be better understood if we realized its purpose. The purpose of praise is to glorify God (Harper Collins Study Bible 1985). He is worthy to be praised! It is easy to praise the Lord when things are going right. The question is can we praise God when the devil is on our track. It is important to praise God in all situations, even in those times when we experience spiritual warfare (Psalm 34:1). Praise is an assault weapon against Satan. When evil comes, praise the Lord; not for the evil, but as a declaration of war against it. Every believer, who praises the Lord, can and will bind the powers of darkness.

THEOLOGICAL FOUNDATION

My theological reflections tell me that this project is significant because God's goal for believers is to be equipped and empowered for spiritual warfare. Scripture clearly confirms that Satan is the enemy of every human being, and in our power we are unprepared to stand victorious against satanic attacks. Many believers shy away from any discussion about spiritual warfare, Satan, and demons. Because of fear, believers today choose to ignore this adversary and hope Satan will ignore the people of God. This approach to the study of Satan is unbiblical and has left many Christians open prey to wicked attacks.

Believers are falling victim to Satan's attack feeling defeated, frustrated, and are living in bondage to sin. The church must prepare the people of God to stand firm against Satan's attack by equipping them to understand spiritual warfare and to identify and effectively use God's armor. What are the theological themes that are born out of this project? What are the major themes around my topic?

What have theologians written about spiritual warfare? Is Satan real and do Satanic attacks exist today? Does Satan always seek to do evil? How have theologians contributed to our understanding of spiritual warfare? Neill k. Foster holds a PH.D in intercultural studies, said:

> "About the levels where human authority exists, there is a spiritual realm occupied by spiritual forces. There are spirit beings who, through the fall of man in Eden, have gained a place where they are able to dominate men" (Foster 1995, 114).

The doctrine of Spiritual Warfare is a prominent theme throughout this project. Spiritual warfare is the invisible confrontation between the forces of God and the forces of the devil, and the kingdom of God versus the kingdom of darkness. Edward Murphy, author of *The Handbook for Spiritual Warfare,* is of the opinion that spiritual warfare is the most perplexing problem ever challenged by the church/humanity (Murphy 1996, 17). Unlike earthly warfare, spiritual warfare involves fighting an invisible enemy. Sometimes, the battle brings about circumstances that can hurt humans physically, emotionally, mentally, or spiritually (2 Kings 6:15-18).

Spiritual warfare is a way of characterizing our Christians' common struggle between the forces of Satan and the forces of God. Whether we want to believe it, deny it, or question its reality, the truth is that we all face supernatural opposition as we set out to live the Christian life. We have an opponent who wants nothing more than to bring about our demise. Satan wants to hinder our every effort to share the good news of liberation with those still held in captivity. Fred C. Dickason states:

> "At the same time, the Bible presents God as both omnipotent and sovereign. He is in control of all things and He has no potential successful rival (Isaiah 41: 4; 43: 13; 45:5; 46:8-11; Ephesians 1: 11; Revelation 4:11). Evil did not rise up apart from His control; otherwise He would no longer be God" (Dickason 1995, 143)

From the perspective of the Hebrew people, spiritual warfare was a holy war that God Himself declared, led, and won. The concept was at its height during the period of the Judges. By the time of the United Kingdom under David and Solomon, however, political concerns began to cloud the concept of holy war. The prophets saw war as God's judgment against Israel. Those looking for a violent end to human existence saw war as a sign of the end of time, both in the Old and New Testaments.

Spiritual warfare shines a spotlight of truth on the basic problem of human existence and human history. Paul Hiebert professor of Mission and Anthropology at Trinity Evangelical Divinity School in Deerfield, Illinois said:

> For most tribal people, ancestors, earthly spirits, witchcraft, and magic are very real. The people see the earth and sky as full of beings (gods, earthly divinities, ancestors, ghosts, evil shades, humans, animals, and nature spirits) that relate, deceive, bully, and battle one another for power and personal gain. These beings are neither totally good nor totally evil. They help those who serve or placate them. They harm those who oppose their wishes or who neglect them or refuse to honor them. Humans must placate them to avoid terrible disasters. (Hiebert 2006, 2)

Paul Hiebert continues that the battle between good and evil is discovered all religions. He said:

> Battles between good and evil and of power encounters between good gods and evil demons are found in all religions. In Hinduism Rama battles Ravana, in Buddhism Buddha fights

Mara, in Islam Allah wars against Shaitan, and in traditional religions tribal gods fight one another for conquest. (Hiebert 2006, 1)

The Christian Church believes that Satan and demons are spiritual entities that exist and sometimes manifest their presence in the world. The primary focus of these entities is the spiritual deception of humanity. Their primary mission is to thwart God's purposes on earth and specifically prevent non-believers from placing their faith in Christ Jesus and prevent Christians from being effective disciples of Jesus (Wardle 2004, 2). Satan is referred to as "the father of lies" (John 8:44) and as "the accuser of our brothers" (Rev. 12:10). Jesus emphasized peace instead of war, and the New Testament church saw war as a spiritual warfare or battle between good and evil.

In spiritual warfare, Satan looks for areas of weaknesses in our lives and seeks ways to exploit and deceive us. Charles Kraft and Mark White, co-authors of *Behind Enemy Lines: An Advanced Guide to Spiritual Warfare,* view spiritual warfare as multidimensional with demonization being on the ground level. They define the ground-level as the direct effects of demonic beings on humans, such as temptation to sin, demonic harassment, oppression, and demonization (demons inhabiting people) (Kraft and White 2000, 65).

Today, the study of spiritual warfare is too frightening for many Christians. However, to ignore this enemy and hope he will quietly go away is both unrealistic and hazardous. *Born for Battle,* written by Arthur Mathews states:

> The terrifying face of a hostile world of evil and malicious spirit paralyzes many Christians into inactivity and unwillingness to seek out biblical answers and to apply them. There re many clear indications of Satan's motives and methods given to us in the Bible, if only we would heed them. His central purpose is to pull God from His throne in the minds of humans and to take that throne himself. (Mathews 1992, 127)

Many Christians have misunderstood the concept of spiritual warfare as the right and authority to exercise power of the adversary whenever and however they decide. They erroneously assume victory in warfare always means the immediate removal of Satan or squelching his plans. There are also Christians who grasp only half the truth about spiritual warfare. By grasping only half the truth, many Christians in error assume because we are God's children we are immune from warfare. When warfare occurs, Christians can always rebuke, bind or cast out Satan to get relief. Is Satan real and do satanic attacks exist today? Does Satan always seek to do evil?

Satan is real and understanding the doctrine of Satan is a prominent theme in this project. Satan is evil, and he seeks to do evil. Satan desires that which is wrong, corrupt, and perverse. In the New Testament, the forces of darkness knew that the Apostle Paul was God's servant and they attacked him (Acts 19:14-16). B. J. Oropeza states:

> Too often we abuse the subject spiritual warfare. Some look for demons in every struggle they experience. They spend their time rebuking demons in prayer, imagining themselves on the frontlines of demonic attack. It is important to remember that apart from the Devil and his demons, we also have conflicts with our weak, sinful nature and the influence of fallen people in a fallen world, which is cause enough for the majority of our problems. (Oropeza 1997, 114)

From a theological perspective, it is clear that Satan built his stronghold in the lives of individuals and families. Strongholds have also been built in many churches because the people of God approach the church and life in general with a worldly way of thinking rather than a spiritual mindset. Satan attempts to gain ground in the Church of Jesus Christ and erect strongholds that hinder the work of God. Stronghold is a mindset that accepts as inevitable or unchangeable something that is contrary to the revealed will of God. It is a way of thinking that declares "I can't" when God says "You can." Clinton E. Arnold states:

> "Spiritual Warfare is not just defensive; it is offensive. We have a mission to accomplish. It is best summed up by Jesus' final word as recorded in Matthew's Gospel 28: 18-20" (Arnold 2003, 49)

Arnold also said that the powerful and evil emissaries of the devil need to be resisted with the powerful armor of God (Arnold 1989, 68).

Paul wrote to the Corinthian church declaring that demons attack the mind to gain a foothold in the lives of people. Satan blinds the minds of the unsaved taking them away from the light of the Gospel (2 Cor. 4:3-4). To resist demon influence, one must guard against what he or she reads and what sort of television he permits himself to view. If we are not careful, demon influence may merge into demon obsession. If not curbed, demon invasion may ultimately come about.

Satan seeks to blind our minds to the truth through lies and deception. He tempts Christians with the pleasures of sin and intimidates us with fear by sending misfortunes. Above all, Satan entices the worship of earthly things and promotes a love of self above love for God (Gen. 3:1-7; 2 Tim. 3:2). Charles Kraft and Mark White said, "One of Satan's primary tactics to thwart God's plans is to get God's people to disobey him or to neglect their relationship with him. This the enemy does most effectively through either keeping people ignorant of what God desires (2 Cor. 4:4) or by deceiving them into disobeying (Gen. 3:1-7) (Kraft and White 2000, 47)."

The sin problem has three major dimensions. First of all, sin is personal; it comes from within as we engage in warfare with the flesh. Secondly, sin is social; it comes from without as we engage in warfare with the world around us. Thirdly, sin is supernatural; it comes from above as we engage in warfare with Satan's invisible cosmic kingdom of evil made up of Satan himself and all the demonic hierarchy under his command (Eph. 6:10-20). I call this third area "evil supernaturalism." It is the main focus of ground-level spiritual warfare (Kraft and White 2000, 65-66).

The sin nature of the flesh, which is a daily battle, is not the same as the old self that once controlled life and is now permanently crucified with Christ (Gal. 2:20). Before coming to Christ, life was dominated by a sinful nature inherited from Adam, separated from God and spiritually dead. This was the old man or old self. Jesus took the old man self with Him to the cross. It died with Him there. Apostle Paul affirms, "Know this, that our old self was crucified with Him" (Rom. 6:6). Paul says, "Set your mind on the things above, not on the things that are on earth. For you have died and your life is hidden with Christ in God" (Gal. 3:2-3).

The devil is continually active, roaming in the shadows, looking for vulnerable prey. He does not stop his activity. Christians should not stop or avoid the tasks appointed by God, but claim the protection God offers from the enemy's forces. We must also claim protection for their families, property, and themselves. In addition, seek and embrace righteousness, faith, salvation, prayer, the sword of the Spirit, and the Word of God. I concur with Gregory Boyd, who is of the opinion,

> Philosophical theology believes all things must ultimately follow a divine blueprint that is, in detail, foreknown and willed by God. Thus whether we speak of God ordaining or allowing the evil to occur, there must always be a divine purpose for it occurring. It is decreed by God because all things work together for good. (Boyd 1997, 39)

Before coming to Christ, life was dominated by a sinful nature inherited from Adam, separated from God and spiritually dead. This was the old man or old self. Jesus took the old man with Him to the cross. Our sins were nailed to the cross and died with Him there. Paul affirms, "For we know that our old self was crucified with Him..." (Rom. 6:6). Paul continued, "Set your mind on the things above, not on earthly things. For you died, and your life is now hidden with Christ in God" (Col. 3:2-3). The sin nature of the flesh, which is a daily battle, is not the same as the old self that once controlled life and is now permanently crucified with Christ. The devil most often does not attack through obvious head-on assaults, but uses cunning strategies specifically designed to trick believers of Christ unaware.

What Christians discover about themselves and God's will is critically important to the process of spiritual warfare and change. In this process of discovery, the Christians allow the Spirit of Christ to redeem and recreate him or her in very deep and important ways. James, the brother of Jesus, instructs Christians to "Submit yourselves, then, to God. Resist the devil, and he will flee from you" (James 4:7). There are many ways to resist Satan. The most explicit passage on spiritual warfare is found in Ephesians 6:10-20. Discernment, wisdom, and common sense go a long way in this war for the devil seldom shows his true colors in an attack. Christian strength does not come from within, but from God's mighty power. Paul believes that the Lord's servants must put on the entire armor of God. One piece of the armor is the sword of the Spirit.

The doctrine of the Holy Spirit is a prominent theme throughout this project. The presence of God within the believer inspires and empowers us with qualities we would not otherwise possess. The Holy Spirit (Hebrew, *ruach;* Greek, *pneuma)* works within us, He blesses us, and transforms us. The Holy Spirit is our source of inspiration and power. He is the vehicle of God's revelation and activity who gives us wisdom, courage, and power to stand boldly and confidently against the devil's schemes and tricks. "The Spirit makes Christians one 'in Christ' and empowers them, not only for the mission of the church, but also for the moral and ethical life appropriate to those who understand themselves to be people of the new age" (Achtemeier 1985, 401). God's spirit gives believers the courage to take decisive action.

The Holy Spirit is important to the process of spiritual warfare and change. The Scriptures reveal the Holy Spirit is one who comforts, rebukes, corrects, and trains Christians in righteousness. It is therefore essential to be thoroughly equipped with the Scriptures and the Holy Spirit to be prepared for every good work. The better equipped we are for spiritual warfare, the more effective we will be in our spiritual journey.

In spiritual warfare, after Christians have received the Holy Spirit's empower, we are commanded to imitate Jesus' obedience and intimate relationship with the Father. Our relationship with Him will enable us to follow Jesus' example in warfare against the kingdom of Satan. Paul said having done all you can to stand, stand in the power of God's might with the armor God has made available to us (Eph. 6:10-18). He exhorts all believers to put on the shield of faith, the breastplate of righteousness, the helmet of salvation, feet shod with the gospel of peace, and carry the sword of the spirit which is the Bible. Paul concludes the full armor by encouraging Christians to pray in the Spirit.

When Christians pray in the Holy Spirit, they will find the authority and power for a substantial defense in spiritual warfare. Why is prayer in the Spirit so important? Often, Christians do not know what to pray for, so the Spirit Himself intercedes with groans that words cannot express but are known and understood by God (Rom. 8:26). When praying in the Spirit, Christians must be immersed in the environment of the Spirit. In 1 Corinthians 2: 9-13, Paul shows what it means to be in a Holy Spirit environment when he states:

> Eyes have not seen and ears have not heard, no mind has conceived what God has prepared for those who love Him- but God has revealed it to us by His Spirit. The Spirit searches all things, even the deep things of God. For who among men knows the thoughts of a man except the man's spirit within him? In the same way no one knows the thoughts of God except the Spirit who is from God, that we may understand what God has freely given us. This is what we speak, not in words taught by human wisdom but in words taught by the Spirit, expressing spiritual truths in spiritual words.

When Christians pray in the Spirit, we enter into a whole other realm. We enter into the heavenlies and are shown life and its challenges from a different perspective. Praying through the Holy Spirit, the Spirit of Truth, will bring enlightenment, empowerment, and the manifestation of God's presence to every area of our lives (1 Cor. 2:10-16). Prayer is necessary because the battle is spiritual and characterized by resistance in the heavenly realm.

Does spiritual warfare exist today? Certainly! Biblical scholars agree that a spiritual battle is going on in this world.

> Wiersbe said, "The important point is that our battle is not against human beings. It is against spiritual powers. We are wasting our time fighting people when we ought to be fighting the devil who seeks to control people and make them oppose the work of God (Wiersbe 1997, 554).

Satan is at war with every believer and seeks to disturb the lives of Christians so they do not live as true children of God. The moment we trusted and accepted the Lord Jesus Christ as our personal Savior, we learned that spiritual warfare became a part of our life's struggle.

However, we must remember God is the only one who is all powerful; Satan is not. Whenever Satan perpetrates evil against the children of God, God uses that evil to accomplish His will. God can also turn into good what Satan means for evil. Through Jesus Christ we can stand triumphant in spiritual conflict. We know God lives in the believer and the believer lives in God. Thus we know and rely on the love God has for His children. With faith in God and identifying and using God's armor, we are equipped to become more than conquerors against spiritual warfare.

Eugene Peterson states:

> Warfare is an important metaphor on scripture and we must take it seriously. Eugene Peterson writes, 'There is a spiritual war in progress, an all-out moral battle. There is evil and cruelty, unhappiness and illness. There is superstition and ignorance, brutality and pain. God is in continuous and energetic battle against all of it. God is for life and against death. God is for love and against hate. God is for hope and against despair. God is for heaven and against hell. There is no neutral ground in the universe. Every square foot of space is contested. (Peterson 1997, 122-123)

Many Christians may have misunderstood the concept of spiritual warfare as the right and authority to exercise power over the adversary whenever and however they decide. By grasping only half the truth, many Christians mistakenly assume the following:

1. Victory in warfare always means the immediate removal of Satan or squelching his plans.

2. Christians are immune from warfare.

3. When warfare occurs, Christians can always rebuke/bind/cast out Satan to get relief.

Does the war still exist today? Certainly! Satan is at war with the offspring of the woman (Rev. 12:7-17). Whenever Satan perpetrates evil against the children of God, God uses that evil to accomplish His will.

God turns into good what Satan means for evil and remains triumphant in this spiritual conflict.

Satan and other fallen beings, now known as demons, are spiritual entities that exist and sometimes manifest their presence in the world. These entities have as their primary focus the spiritual deception of humanity. Their primary mission is to thwart God's purposes on earth, specifically to prevent non-believers from placing faith in Christ and to prevent Christians from being effective disciples of Jesus. Satan is referred to as "the father of lies" (John 8:44) and as "the accuser of our brothers" (Rev. 12:10).

Eugene H. Peterson states:

> The biblical answer is clear, even though how it could occur is nowhere explained. Satan is the father of lies because he is himself a liar. Jesus affirms. He lied both to the angels and to humanity because he was already a liar. Furthermore, Jesus declares that "He was a murderer from the beginning" John 8: 44; ct. 1 John 3: 8. (Peterson 1992, 31)

If Christians pray in the Holy Spirit, they will find the authority and power for a substantial defense in spiritual warfare. Why is prayer in the Spirit so important? Often, Christians do not know what to pray for, so the Spirit Himself intercedes with groans that words cannot express but are known and understood by God (Rom. 8:26).

> Spiritual warfare points to the final establishment of the Kingdom of God throughout the whole universe. When we focus too much on the current battle, we lose sight of the cosmic picture in which the real story is-not the battle, but the eternal reign of Christ. That vision transformed the early Church, and should be our focus in ministry today. (Kaiser, 1996, 10)

The most important issue in the spiritual warfare discussion has to do with the cross. Jesus has given the sign of the cross as a reminder to live harmoniously in the world. The Christian cross symbolizes the four areas of a balanced life: mental health, physical health, spiritual health, and social health. Followers of Christ strive to maintain holistic balance in their lives by applying biblical truths to the everyday challenges they encounter. Praying through the Holy Spirit, the Spirit of Truth, will bring enlightenment, empowerment, and the manifestation of God's presence to every area of our lives (1 Cor. 2:10-16). Prayer is necessary because the battle is spiritual and characterized by resistance in the heavenly realm.

Satan would like to blind the minds of humans to the truth through lies and deception. Satan tempts Christians with the pleasures of sin. He intimidates with fear by sending misfortunes. Above all, he entices the worship of earthly things and promotes a love of self above love for God (Gen. 3: 1-7; 2 Tim. 3:2).

HISTORICAL RATIONALE

The previous sections have examined what many Old and New Testament Biblical Scholars had to say about the need for Christians to be equipped for spiritual warfare. The previous sections also examined the theological themes portrayed throughout this project and what many theologians had to say understanding spiritual warfare as well as effectively use the armor of God.

The entire biblical account, from Genesis to the Revelation, expresses the ongoing conflict between good and evil. Similarly, historically, the Church has discovered and concluded that spiritual warfare exists in the universe. What do historians have to say about spiritual warfare? From a historical perspective, who is Satan; what does Satan do; what are the resources God has provided; and what is our responsibility when encountering satanic attack?

Spiritual warfare

All of human history and all human divine encounters have taken place in the context of spiritual warfare. It is acknowledged that God created moral beings who obeyed His will and were able to coexist peaceably. However, this harmony did not last. "At some point in the hidden past rebellion occurred within the angelic kingdom, the Kingdom of God and the Kingdom of Satan" (Murphy 1996, 13).

Historians have found references to spiritual warfare throughout the ages. Philosopher Lactantius, who lived between 260-340 A.D., quoted a statement believed to be written by Greek philosopher Epicurus between 341-270 B.C.:

> God either wishes to take away evils and is unable; or he is able and unwilling; or he is neither willing nor able, or he is both willing and able. If he is willing and is unable, he is feeble, which is not in accordance with the character of God; if he is able and unwilling, he is envious, which is equally at variance with God; if he is neither willing nor able, he is both envious and feeble, and therefore not God; if he is both willing and able, which alone is suitable to God, from what source then are evils? Or why does he not remove them? (Murphy 1996, 17)

In the eighteenth century, early Christian tradition indicates that Gnosticism had its roots as far back at least to the Qumran community with its theology of cosmic conflict between good and evil. Gnostics claimed possession of a special knowledge and held to the belief that the created world is evil and is totally separate from and in opposition to the world of spirit (Murphy 1996, 18). Still, it is believed that the most complex and profound dimension of spiritual warfare has to do with the origin of the conflict. Spiritual warfare did not originate on earth with the fall of man, but happened somewhere and sometime in the heavenly realm.

Spiritual warfare is an integral part of the entire Christian experience. It is a fact of life. Our goals, as believers, should be to gain an accurate and sober-minded understanding of spiritual warfare. Our goal also should be not to be led astray by a tainted view originating from frightening superstitions and odd practices. Clinton Arnold explains,

> Christians are in the midst of a struggle that is far greater than us, but it is not bigger than our God. It involves two warring kingdoms, but the sides are not at all evenly matched. There is no cosmic dualism here, with two

opposing gods of near-equal power. The testimony of
scripture from beginning to end is that Yahweh is
sovereign. He created everything in heaven and earth. All
of the spiritual powers derive their life from him. He (God)
holds them in the palm of his hand, and can do with them
as He will. In fact, He has already revealed the final
outcome of the battle. Christians are on the winning side
(Arnold 2003, 23).

Does God have a purpose for spiritual warfare?

Gregory Boyd is of the opinion that there is a divine purpose for the evil that enters one's life (Boyd 1997, 39). While the evil itself may be against God's will, He is all-knowing and will orchestrate circumstances for the ultimate good of mankind. God is able to turn every circumstance around for the long-range good of humanity. God has allowed all individuals to choose which influence to follow.

> Human sin always has a dual source. It has a human source,
> one's wrong choices. But it also has a supernatural source,
> Satan's temptations. He plants the seed of evil thoughts and
> imaginations into human minds and hearts, intensifying the
> evil already there. (Murphy 1996, 19)

The Apostle Paul reminds us that all things, good and bad, work for the good of those who are the called of God (Rom. 8:28).

Although warfare in itself is not evil, spiritual warfare is an evil issue. Evil is prevalent in our contemporary, fallen world. Gregory Boyd states:

> The figure Satan continues to permeate the thinking of the
> Church in other respects throughout history, at least up
> until the time of the Enlightenment. As was said, the
> Church retained at least an echo of the warfare worldview.
> But in terms of arriving at an ultimate explanation for evil,
> after Augustine, the question always gets filed under the

category of God's providence instead of under the category of spiritual warfare, that is, under the topic of what Satan, rebel angels, and fallen humans freely choose to do against God's will. With Augustine, it becomes a problem of understanding evil as part of God's will. (Boyd 1997, 55)

Satan

Satan and his demons came to represent the powers of evil in the universe. The hosts of Satan are committed to hinder and obstruct the work of Christ. Demons are always opposed to God's purposes and God's people. Robert Baker Girdlestone describes Satan (שָׂטָן) as an adversary or plotter, or one who devises means for opposing another (Girdlestone 1998, 288).

Augustus Strong regards Satan as a collective term for all evil beings, human or superhuman. He said,

> The Scripture representations of the progressive rage of the great adversary, from his first assault on human virtue in Genesis to his final overthrow in Revelation, join with the testimony of Christ just mentioned, to forbid any other conclusion than this, that there is a personal being of great power, who carries on organized opposition to the divine government. (Strong 2004, 447)

Satan is also called an adversary. *In The Tyndale Dictionary* an adversary is defined as any foe, opponent, or enemy of God and his people. "The Apostle Peter's description of the devil as "your adversary" (1 Pet. 5:8) has led to use of 'the adversary' as a reference to Satan in literature and popular speech" (Elwell 2001, 19). Satan is a strong enemy and evil is thriving in our society, yet we know God will stand with us and fight against the schemes of the devil.

Gregory Boyd, author of *God at War,* is of the opinion that. God's righteousness can be worn as our breastplate to protect us from Satan's temptations.

For Christians, a spiritual life is the everyday actualization of what is sacramentally given in the Church. I believe it is therefore a continual act of communion with God. Spiritual warfare also has an impact on Church life. The apostle Paul told Timothy to watch out for 'doctrines of demons' that will infiltrate the Church....Spiritual warfare affects the life of a nation, the culture in which we live. (Boyd 1997, 23)

Satan's Strategy

Satan desires to lead us into temptation that will result in the Christian falling short of God's glory. The author of *Paul, The Missionary Apostle* in is study of Paul's life discovered the following:

While sin looks inviting, it does not take long before sin takes away your ability to control your life. Sin takes away your ability to control your life. Sin takes away our strength and leaves us helpless before the consequences of evil. (Butler 1997, 735)

John Butler concluded that sin begets sin; one sin encourages another sin and makes it easier to sin more. Moreover, yielding to a temptation makes it easier to yield to future sins. We must beware because evil snowballs if not stopped by the grace of God (Butler 1997, 22).

In the Calvin Theological Journal (CTJ) Robert Me Fee Brown wrote in an article entitled Patterns of Faith that "Sin is fundamentally a description of entire situation, one of separation from God, alienation from him, arising out of our rebellion, our refusal to do his will, our insistence upon following our own walk" (Brown 1967, 132). I agree with Brown, sin persists because we alienate ourselves from God (Brown 1967, 138).

My personal experience with temptation and sin leads me to agree with Peter Gomes, author of *The Scandalous Gospel of Jesus: What's So Good About the Good News. He said,*

The temptations (of Jesus) point out the fact that Satan

usually appeals to us at the point where we feel ourselves spiritually strong, for where we think we are strong is not the place in which we invest our defensive energies (Gomes 2007, 33).

Some Christians have misunderstood the whole spiritual warfare concept. Spiritual beings who object to earthly activities are said to cause evil, disaster, and chaos. These are commonly referred to as evil spirits or demons. On April 5, 1991, Americans were given the opportunity to watch an exorcism performed live on "20/20," an ABC television program. This viewing prompted Barbara Walters to ask, "Is the devil real" (Oropeza 1997, 13). Yes, the devil is real, but his powers have been limited. This is the hour when it appears that darkness reigns. However, the death, burial, and resurrection of Christ assure us that we are more than conquerors.

I concur with Gomes, conflict is a reality; it is the way of the world and is the persistence of evil in the world (Gomes 2007, 119). Gomes said, "Conflict is an unavoidable part of the world in which believers must live. The question is not how to avoid conflict but how to engage in it with the least amount of damage" (Gomes 2007, 119). God has provided resources for our confrontations with the continual evil in the world.

What are the resources God has provided?

God's Resources: the armor of God

The armor of God strengthens and enables us to resist the diabolic "powers" of darkness. When we are equipped with the armor of God, we are enabled to resist enemy aggression. In addition, we can maintain the ground which rightfully belongs to one who is in Christ (Arnold 1989, 119). He concludes that "each of the material weapons used as metaphors depict some aspect of divine strength" (Arnold 1989, 110).

Prayer is an essential spiritual weapon. Arnold said, "Pray for inner strengthening through the Holy Spirit and the indwelling Christ who roots the life of a believer in love and for a personal knowledge of power and love of God" (Arnold 1989, 86). "In Ephesians 6:18-20 prayer is seen as essential to the army of believers with the power of God in order to resist the diabolic powers who would seek to prevent them from living according to Christian ethics" (Arnold 1989, 112).

The Holy Spirit is a gift from God whose ministry includes empowering us to resist the continuing powerful influence of evil forces through spiritual warfare we must rely on the power of the Holy Spirit. The presence and power of God does indeed work in and on our behalf against the backdrop of hostile spiritual powers. "The divine power is provided to the believer for a specific purpose--- that the influences and attacks of the evil forces might be successfully resisted" (Arnold 1989, 121). The power of God will enable us to "stand against the wiles of the devil," "resist in the evil day," and quench the flaming arrows of the evil one."

By faith we can put on the full armor of God. By faith we can seek the Lord in prayer and ask for whatever we need. In the midst of the struggle between right and wrong, we can trust God to make available the resources we need to experience against Satan. By faith we can depend on God to give us the strength we need. Arnold contends that "Faith is the means to acquiring divine strength" (Arnold 1989, 111). Moreover, faith says Arnold, is essential to gaining access to the power of God in order to engage in spiritual warfare (Arnold 1989, 111). By faith we can trust God to equip us for spiritual warfare. Historians remind us that spiritual warfare is a lifelong spiritual battle and we must understand it and effectively use the armor God has provided.

CONCLUSION

Spiritual Warfare is an evil attempt initiated by Satan to deceive and control the people of God. Evil is the most perplexing problem ever faced by humanity. We are saved by the blood of the lamb, but our ultimate redemption awaits us in the future. As long as we are in this world, we are exposed to temptations, and need to be on our watch against them. It is the church's responsibility to equip every believer for spiritual warfare. It is also expedient that we teach Christians how to stand fast in the assurance of our faith, enduring to the end. No matter how strongly Satan tries, he cannot snatch anyone away from God if our faith is unwavering. We have the blessed assurance that God will never leave us nor forsake us.

The Bible records evidence about cosmic rebellion against the rule of God by frequent references to evil in the guise of supernatural beings who seek to injure humans and lead them away from a life of obedience to God. The spiritual forces of evil and the powers of this dark world are not to be underestimated. Our battle is not against human beings. It is against spiritual powers orchestrated by the devil who seeks to control people and make them oppose the work of God. In response to this evil, we must arm ourselves with the full armor of God. Only then will we be able to quench all the fiery darts of the wicked.

In faith we believe Jesus defeated the principalities and power on the Cross. Jesus' incarnation, death on the cross, and resurrection permanently changed human history. Jesus' shed blood has sealed the ultimate doom of Satan and his demonic power. We can enjoy our new life in Jesus Christ, because we have joined Him in His death and resurrection. Because He defeated Satan, we too can experience victory over Satan.

Chapter Three will review the literature and ministry that provide support to the relevance of this project. Major themes and key issues will be discussed. Components of God's armor will be identified, and current models and practices relating to spiritual warfare will be explored.

CHAPTER THREE

REVIEW OF THE LITERATURE

For the foundation of the classical philosophical portrait of God's relationship to the world is the conviction that whatever happens must somehow fit into God's sovereign plan. All things must ultimately follow a divine blueprint that is, in detail, foreknown and willed by God. Thus, whether we speak of God "ordaining" or "allowing" the evil to occur, there must always be a divine purpose for it occurring. It is all decreed by God because "all things work together for good" (according to one common interpretation of Romans 8:28). In classical theological thinking, events may occur "against" God's will, but paradoxically they can never occur outside God's will (Boyd 1997, 39).

Satan was made like his Creator, completely free to exercise his will. Satan could do or not do the will of God as he saw fit. He had the power to revolt if he wanted to. It was not suspected that he would covet his maker's throne, for he seemingly held every honor but that. Ezekiel indicates he lived to praise God. But alas, the day came when "iniquity was found" in him. Therefore, it was probably not planned. The answer to that remains locked in God for the time. If spiritual warfare (sin) can be defined as rebellion against the known will of God, sin began that day. (Lovett 1967, 17)

Chapter One provided a general overview of the project, including the purpose, rationale, context and assessment. The purpose of this project was to measure the impact of a six-week course at Unity Baptist Church in Detroit, Michigan on the participants' understanding of spiritual warfare, as well as their identification of and use of God's armor. The project used the following question as a guideline: What is the impact of a six-week course at Unity Baptist Church in Detroit, Michigan in equipping participants to understand spiritual warfare, as well as identify and effectively use God's armor? I answered this question by gathering data from Unity Baptist Church members who participated in the six- week course. The results determined if the participants were equipped in their understanding of spiritual warfare, as well as their ability to identify and effectively use God's armor.

In Chapter Two, I traced the biblical, theological, and historical foundations of concepts such as "spiritual warfare," and "equipping." Pedagogical emphasis was on theology, biblical exegesis, spiritual conflict, and the Presence of God evident in the work of the Holy Spirit. The chapter also provided the participants the opportunity to receive a deeper understanding of spiritual warfare. Chapter Two also presented the participants with the chance to identify each component of God's armor, and they were encouraged to use God's armor in spiritual warfare.

In Chapter Three, the purpose is to review the literature that relates to the necessity of understanding spiritual warfare and the available armor God provides every believer. The review also includes current and historical issues as they relate to spiritual conflict and the resources God provides for victorious living. The literature explains and justifies why Christians should prepare for encountering dark forces and why they should protect themselves with spiritual armor.

This chapter is divided into the following four sections: the field of study, major theories, models and practices, and application. To confirm the extent to which equipping Christians for spiritual warfare can enhance their ability to stand against Satan the following questions will be discussed: What are contemporary writers saying about the reality of Satan? What are contemporary writers saying about spiritual warfare? What role do demons play in spiritual warfare? What are the resources God has provided to equip Christians to effectively stand against Satan?

THE FIELD OF STUDY

The Reality of Satan

What are contemporary writers saying about the reality of Satan?

Is Satan real? Yes! Satan is real and the foe of every human being starting with Adam and Eve. Spiritual warfare is real. To ignore this enemy and his strategies and hope he will ignore us is both unrealistic and hazardous. According to Tony Evans, "Spiritual warfare is that conflict being waged in the invisible, spiritual realm that is being manifest in the visible, physical realm..." (Evans 1998, 19). The battle between the invisible, angelic forces and the physical forces affect you and me. Living out our personal relationship with God includes spiritual warfare. Although warfare in itself is not evil, spiritual warfare is an evil issue. Edward Murphy said, "Evil is the most perplexing problem ever faced by humanity" (Murphy 1996, 17).

What is the assignment of evil spiritual forces?

Evil spiritual forces constantly are encouraging undesirable tendencies within Christians, such as pride, lust, envy, anger, lying, and rage. Satan attempts to influence spiritual minds to mimic these behaviors.
In Romans 7:21-23, Apostle Paul wrote:

> So I find this law at work: When I want to do good, evil is right there with me. For in my inner [spirit] being I delight in God's law; but I see another law at work in the members of my body, waging war against the law of my [spirit] mind and making me a prisoner of the law of sin at work within my members.

According to Charles Ryrie author of *A Survey of Bible Doctrine,*

> Satan's avowed purpose is to thwart the plan of God in every area and by every means possible. To accomplish this, he is promoting a world system of which he is the

> head and which stands in opposition to God and His rule in this universe. However, instead of promoting a kingdom whose characteristics are exactly opposite to the features of God's rule, he seeks to counterfeit God's program. Counterfeiting, of course, has a single purpose, and that is to create something as similar to the original as possible and to do it by means of a shortcut. (Ryrie 1995)

Does Satan have a kingdom from which he plans his attacks?

Satan's kingdom is viewed by some as only a vapor composed of the darkness in which he resides. Others believe that Satan has an actual kingdom. Ed Tarkowski, in his understanding of Daniel 2:35, believes "there are two kingdoms set up visibly in the last of days, the kingdom of darkness and the Kingdom of God" (Tarkowski 2007, 4). According to scripture, the kingdom of darkness is in the hearts of men (Luke 11:18). "The Kingdom of God is within each of us now, because of God's mercy and grace and our faith in Him and His word" (Rom. 14:17). If Satan is divided against himself, how can his kingdom stand?

> There is no hope at all for the triumph of the kingdom of darkness - none at all. They'll either be in the lake of fire with Satan and all those in his kingdom (or realm) of darkness, or with God in the Kingdom He prepared before creation for those who love Him with their whole being because of His Spirit in their hearts. (Ed Tarkowski 2007, 10)

We are merely weak humans and the use of human methods and carnal weapons will not give us victory in our battles against Satan. We need divine help to deal with the devil's attacks. God, our heavenly Father, who dwells in heavenly places, is the only one who can help us in spiritual battles. To stand victorious against Satan, we must identify and use the resources God has provided.

Spiritual Warfare

What are contemporary writers saying about spiritual warfare?

Spiritual warfare is a prominent theme of this project because believers either ignore the reality of Satan or underestimate his influence in our lives. Spiritual warfare means different things to different people. Spiritual warfare is conflict originating in the invisible, spiritual realm that is also evident in the visible, physical realm. It refers both to the believer's multidimensional war against personal sin and the warfare with Satan and his fallen angels. Satan is a strong enemy. He attempts to defeat us with an array of evil strategies and through well-laid plans and deliberate deception. According to Dr. Edward Murphy, [author of his works] spiritual warfare is the most perplexing problem ever faced by humanity (Murphy 1996, 17).

The term itself, spiritual warfare is not found in the scriptures; however, the Bible does confirm that Christians are in a war. Unlike earthly warfare, spiritual warfare involves fighting an invisible enemy. The Apostle Paul addresses the reality of Satan and spiritual warfare in his letters to the Ephesians and Corinthian churches (Eph. 6:10-12; 2 Cor. 10:3-5). A careful study of Paul's letters to the church informs us that our warfare is not with human beings but with the devil and his demons.

D. R. W. Wood in the New Bible Dictionary defined spiritual warfare and wrote,

> to emphasize that Christians (and even archangels, Jude 9) are engaged in a conflict that is both relentlessly and cunningly waged. They are not in a position to retire from the conflict. Nor can they simply assume that evil will always be obviously evil. There is need for the exercise of discrimination as well as stout-heartedness. But determined opposition will always succeed. Peter urges his readers to resist the devil 'firm in your faith' (1 Pet. 5:9), and James says, 'Resist the devil and he will flee from you' (Jas. 4:7). Paul exhorts 'give no opportunity to the devil' (Eph. 4:27), and the implication of putting on the whole armor of God is that thereby the believer will be able to resist anything the

evil one does (Eph. 6:11,13). Paul puts his trust in the faithfulness of God. 'God is faithful, and he will not let you be tempted beyond your strength, but with the temptation will also provide the way of escape' (1 Cor. 10:13). He is well aware of the resourcefulness of Satan, and that he is always seeking to 'gain the advantage over us'. But he can add 'we are not ignorant of his designs' (or, as F. J. Rae translates, 'I am up to his tricks') (2 Cor. 2:11). (Wood1996, 1064)

Demons

What role do demons play in spiritual warfare?

According to William Evans, the origin of demons is not revealed in the Bible. However, they are thought to be angels who fell with Satan (Matt. 25:41; Rev. 12:7, 9). Similar to Satan, demons attempt to thwart the purpose of God in every way possible (Dan 10:10-14; Rev 16:13-16). According to William Evans, the origin of demons is not revealed in the Bible. They are thought to be angels who fell with Satan (Matt. 25:41; Rev. 12:7, 9). Satan is their prince, ruling them through an evil hierarchy (Eph. 6:12). Demons are evil, unclean, vicious spirits who seek to possess the bodies of men (Matt. 10:1; Mark 5:1-13) (Evans 1998, 230).

The role demons play in spiritual warfare, like Satan, is to attempt to thwart the purpose of God in every way possible. Charles Ryrie said, "In doing this they extend Satan's activity, and the very number of demons engaged as emissaries of Satan is what makes Satan seem to be omnipresent, though he is not" (Ryrie 1995).

God's Resources

What are the resources God has provided to equip Christians to effectively stand against Satan?

The Armor of God

The resources God has provided us to stand against satanic attack are mighty. God's mighty weapons include the armor of God. Christian warfare (conflict) is preeminently a spiritual warfare for which all the armor necessary to obtain victory has been provided. Therefore, Paul admonishes all Christians to put on the full armor of God because we cannot fight without it (Eph. 6). God's mighty weapons are available to use, as we fight against Satan's stronghold (Life Application Bible 1997, 2497). Clinton Arnold presents the armor of God as the strength of believers which enables Christians to resist the diabolic powers of darkness (Arnold 1989, 110). Arnold said, "Each of the material weapons used as metaphors depict some aspect of divine strength" (Arnold 1989, 110). To oppose the evil forces with which they do battle they need to wear the protection God has supplied. To oppose the evil forces with which they do battle they need to wear the protection God has supplied.

The Presence and ministry of the Holy Spirit

The presence and ministry of the Holy Spirit in the life of the believer is also a valuable resource God has given for victory against the attacks of Satan. The presence of God within the believer inspires and empowers us with resources to stand strong in spiritual warfare. The Holy Spirit says Paul Achtemeier is the mysterious power or presence of God in nature or with individuals and communities, inspiring or empowering them with qualities they would not otherwise possess (Achtemeier 1985, 401).

Paul Enns reveals that the Holy Spirit empowers. He said, "The Holy Spirit enables believers to live by His power (Gal. 5:16)" (Enns 1997, 108).

Spiritual Disciplines

Another resource God has provided to equip and empower Christians to effectively stand against Satan is the spiritual disciplines. It is important that Christians practice the disciplines of prayer, study, and meditation. We are encouraged to discipline ourselves in the area of regular devotional times and the reading of the Bible for nourishment and time with God. It is our time with Him that empowers us to stand boldly against the wiles of the devil. Spiritual disciplines and spiritual exercises position Christians for great change and personal transformation.

Richard Foster's book "Celebration of Discipline" teaches us that for the believer, our desire should be to move beyond surface living into deeper depths in Christ. The spiritual disciplines free us to move to another level in Christ (Foster 1998, 2). Developing a rule for daily life provides ministers with a pattern in which to cultivate and deepen their growth into the image of Christ and structure and direction for growth in holiness. Only then can ministers open the door to liberation and experience an enriched spiritual life infused with joy, peace, and a deeper understanding of God (Foster 1998, 2).

When we exercise spiritual disciplines and apply what we have learned and experienced, the indwelling power of the Holy Spirit can actively transform us into the image of Christ. A life lived in the presence of the Lord, is a life of transforming power and victory. Empowered men and women always make a priority of worshipping, serving, and praying consistently.

Faith

It is equally important that we maintain an unwavering faith in God and confidence in His goodness and wisdom. Clinton Arnold contends that "Faith is the means to acquiring divine strength" (Arnold 1989, 111). Moreover, faith says Arnold, is essential to gaining access to the power of God in order to engage in spiritual warfare (Arnold 1989, 111).

In summary, we must believe that God's resources equips and empowers Christians to effectively stand against Satan. Without God's armor, we stand unprepared and helpless against the forces of darkness. The critical battle between good and evil was won by Jesus Christ at Calvary. It is only as we understand spiritual warfare and identify as well as use God's armor that we are assured victory.

THE MAJOR THEORIES

Spiritual warfare is a legitimate concern among all believers regardless of denomination or religious connections. The project focus is for participants to understand the nature of spiritual warfare. In preparation for encounters with the forces of darkness, the aim of this project is to equip Christian individuals with spiritual armor. What is Satan's role in spiritual warfare? What are some of the strategies Satan uses to deceive and control us? What can the church do to equip Christians with God's resources for spiritual warfare? How can spiritual knowledge play a role in equipping Christians for spiritual warfare?

What is Satan's role in spiritual warfare?

Satan's role in the church is to cause confusion and division between the Members, and between the members and the Pastors, Satan seeks to destroy the ministries of the church and to stop the spiritual growth of members. In relation to unbelievers, Satan blinds their minds so that they will not accept the gospel (2 Co 4: 4). We face against a powerful army whose goal is to defeat
Christ's Church.

> The people of God are in a spiritual battle with Satan. There is a spiritual war going on and that spiritual war in the unseen world is driving events in our own visible world. There is no peace in the material world because there is a war now raging in the spiritual world. Why is it that, for all our professed ideals, our hopes, and our skills, peace on earth is still a distant objective seen only dimly through the storms and turmoil of our present difficulties? (Stedman 2007, 10)

What are some of the strategies Satan uses to deceive and control us?

Temptation to Sin

One of the strategies Satan uses to destroy the believer and thwart God's purpose for our lives is through temptation. Our lusts and desires leave us wide open to attacks and influences of Satan and his demons. Unless we know who the enemy is, where he is, and what he can do, we have a difficult time defeating him. Satan is a strong enemy. He does not engage us in open warfare, but deals in wiles and strategies, of which we need to watch against and be prepared. Christians were warned that Satan fights with lies that may sound very much like the truth. We must to arm ourselves with God's truth in order to defeat Satan's lies.

William Evans contends that the Christian's temptations may be said to come from three sources: the world, the flesh, and the devil. Evans said,

> there are temptations which we feel sure come from neither the world nor the flesh, e. g., those which come to us in our moments of deepest devotion and quiet; we can account for them only by attributing them to the devil himself. "That old serpent, the devil, has spoken with fatal eloquence to every one of us no doubt; and I do not need a dissertation from the naturalist on the construction of a serpent's mouth to prove it. Object to the figure if you will, but the grim, damning fact remains." (Evans 1998, 225)

Satan is limited, he is not present everywhere, he is not all-knowing, and he is not all-powerful. Satan has a whole host of evil angels called demons that he can call upon for spiritual evil attacks, but he is not God. Once Satan has established a strong foothold in a person's life (Eph. 4:27), he will often unmask himself to torment and enslave his victim further. Although limited in his knowledge, Satan understands that a corrupted mind will be unable to perceive the will of God. Satan wants the Christian life to be lived in bondage to sin. What is sin?

Sin is, according to D.R.W. Wood, the *New Bible Dictionary*, a violation of that which God's glory demands and is, therefore, in its essence the contradiction of God (New Bible Dictionary, 1996).

According to Freeman in the Anchor Bible Dictionary,

There are three distinguishable although partially overlapping views of sin and sinners: (1) a sin may be an individual wrong act; (2) a sinner may be a person who lives without regard to the will of God and who consequently sins by routine; (3) sin may be conceived as a "power"-some sort of active agent-which opposes God and which can capture humans and make them sinners. (Freedman 1996, 6:41)

Suffering

Satan, demons, evil principalities, and powers are things that frighten a great number of people. Sometimes, this battle brings about circumstances that can hurt humans physically, emotionally, mentally, or spiritually (2 Kings 6:15-18).

The Battlefield of the Mind

One of the major theories of this project is the strategies Satan uses to deceive and defeat us. A powerful tactic Satan uses is the schemes to control our minds. Satan wants control of our minds (Acts 14:2; 2 Cor. 4:4; 11:3). Satan wants to capture our minds because he knows the mind is the leader of all actions. He knows the value in capturing our minds since our actions are a direct result of our thoughts (Acts 14:2; 2 Cor. 4: 4; 11:3). When Satan attacked biblical characters, his main tactic was to subvert their minds. Satan's battle strategy is simple. His strategic plans were designed to deceive God's people and cause them to forget or misunderstand His truth. (Kraft and White 2000, 47) As the father of all lies he endeavored to lead Christians to the wrong conclusions about truth or redirect their focus (John 8:44). Satan is out to deceive us, to trick us into buying his lies and temptations.

The Apostle Paul uses words such as the mind, knowledge, understanding and wisdom many times in his letters. Rev. John D. Tolbert, Senior Pastor of People's Missionary Baptist Church in Detroit, Michigan has given six reasons Satan so desperately wants our minds:

1. The heart is changed by the mind. Just as Jesus sought to change the disciples by enlightening their understanding, Satan wants your mind for his benefits.

2. The mind perceives truth and the will of God. Jesus wanted His followers to understand the truth of scriptures through spiritual understanding. Romans 12:2 tells us our ability to know God's will comes from a transformed mind. The Holy Spirit renews, reeducates, and redirects Christian minds. Satan knows that if he can corrupt our minds, we will be unable to perceive the will of God.

3. The Christian belief system determines direction, actions, and responses. What Christians believe will determine ahead of time their actions and responses. Satan knows that victory for most temptations is not won at the point of the temptation, but usually start with the mind.

4. Unity with God requires a clean mind and heart. Repentance, prayer, God's words, and the Holy Spirit can remove Satan. (Satan doesn't want you to repent.)

5. A corrupted mind will block your usefulness to God in the Kingdom. Even when Christians understand the truth, Satan may at some point influence us enough to turn aside from the right way. (He wants Christians to be corrupted.)

6. The mind is the battlefield for bondage on freedom. Satan knows that if he can deceive us, we will be enslaved. Satan knows the truth will set us free (John 8:32). The mind determines our intimacy with God, our effectiveness as a Christian and our relationship with other behavior. Satan wants our minds. (Tolbert 2006, 7)

We must make our thoughts obedient to Christ because every child of God has been given a promise of victory over Satan. Paul said, "Let the same mind be in you that was in Christ Jesus" (Phil. 2:5 NRSV). If the devil can control our minds he can build a stronghold in our lives. In 2 Corinthians

10:4-5, Paul said the weapons we fight with are not the weapons of this world. On the contrary, they have divine power to demolish strongholds. We demolish arguments and every pretension that sets itself up against the knowledge of God, and we take captive every thought to make it obedient to Christ." It is clear that Satan seeks to build his stronghold in the lives of individuals and families to hinder the work of God.

What are strongholds?

Rev. Tolbert describes a stronghold as follows:

An entrenched pattern of thought, an ideology, value, or behavior that is contrary to the word and will of God or a mindset impregnated with hopelessness that causes Christians to accept as unchangeable situations that Christians know are contrary to the will of God. (Tolbert 2006, 12)

Strongholds have been built in many churches. Satan continually attempts to deceive people into thinking they are worshipping a powerless Savior who can do nothing for them. This would result in a mindset that accepts as inevitable or unchangeable something that is contrary to the revealed will of God. For example, the revealed will of God may be that someone who is ill will be healed after the laying on of hands by the minister; yet Satan's stronghold over that person's life convinces them that they are not and will not be healed. The strategies of Satan confirm the Christians understanding of Satan and spiritual warfare.

What can the church do to equip Christians with God's resources for spiritual warfare?

Spiritual Knowledge

One of the major theories of this project, and one of the tools God offers to help us effectively use God's resources in spiritual warfare is spiritual knowledge. Spiritual knowledge is the God-given ability to understand the Word of God. We can prepare Christians for spiritual warfare through teaching God's Word. When Jesus was confronted with temptation in the wilderness following his baptism, He used the Word of God to combat

Satan (Matt. 4). In order to use the Word of God effectively we must know the Word of God. It is the apprehending of education and wisdom that comes from the presence of God's spirit within. Spiritual knowledge is taught through the Holy Spirit to all believers (Luke 12:12; 1 Cor. 2:13).

According to Randy Frieson, "God's people were religious, yet their religion was not tied to obedience. They had more knowledge of evil than good. Similarly, Christians today can become destroyed through a lack of knowledge" (Frieson 2006, 5). The Apostle Peter said, "for prophesy never came by the will of man, but holy men of God spoke as they were moved by the Holy Ghost" (2 Pet.1:21).

Can Christians be destroyed from a lack of spiritual knowledge?

Yes! True knowledge of Christian authority and power in the spiritual realm flows out of our intimate knowledge of the Father. Christians have been called children of God and are part of His family (John 1:12). He protects us by the power of His name (John 17:11). Can believers under the control of the Holy Spirit have peace on earth from the enemy?

Ray Stedman said:

There is a spiritual war going on and that spiritual war in the unseen world is driving events in our own visible world. There is no peace in the material world because there is a war now raging in the spiritual world. Why is it that, for all our professed ideals, our hopes, and our skills, peace on earth is still a distant objective seen only dimly through the storms and turmoil of our present difficulties? (Stedman 2007, 10)

Stedman continues by stating the Lord Jesus Himself put His finger on the whole problem when He said that Satan's aim is to deceive and destroy God's people. Stedman is of the opinion that, "Because he is a liar and a murderer, the devil's work is to deceive and to destroy. There you have the explanation for all the misery, hatred, murder, war, and other evils that have taken place in human history" (Stedman 2007, 11). Spiritual knowledge reveals that Satan continues to use people to obstruct God's work and one of the areas he attacks is the mind (Gen. 4:8; Rom. 5:12; 1 John 3:12). Spiritual knowledge equips Christians for spiritual warfare revealing the strategy Satan uses to control our minds.

KEY ISSUES

Spiritual warfare is a spiritual matter. We are in a spiritual battle. It is very important to understand the nature of our very existence in order to be able to understand ourselves, spiritual warfare, and how we fit into this cosmic struggle as Christians. The devil does exist and has attacked every believer who was born of a woman. Spiritual warfare continues to be a battle of which Christians should beware. It does not matter whether you want to be in a spiritual battle. We are engaged in spiritual warfare and we are tempted by the devil. I concur with Clinton Arnold, "The concept of spiritual warfare is revealed in the church battling against the forces of evil" (Arnold 1989, 67). Demonic powers are bent on regarding their control in our lives. Believers need to be prepared to engage all the forms of evil in battle (Arnold 1989, 68).

Satan attempts to entrap us in any way he can to keep you from a loving relationship with God. Although it may be very tempting to push the whole subject aside, spiritual warfare must not be ignored. Satan is real. He never gives up and he has a plan of attack. Every Christian is confronted with satanic attack. Charles Stanley, author of *When the Enemy Attacks,* defines a satanic attack as a deliberate, willful, intentional, and well-designed act intended to bring harm to a person. The attack may result in harming an individual physically, mentally, economically, relationally, or spiritually (Stanley 2004, 17). We must actively engage the enemy with the resources God provides. If we do not, Satan has the potential to lead us into spiritual bondage.

The purpose of this project is to equip Christian individuals with the understanding of spiritual warfare, as well as the identification and use of God's armor. Given these challenges, what strategies should Christians use to stand in the midst of spiritual warfare? What is the best approach? What are the components of God's armor?

The Apostle Paul suggests in Eph. 6:10 that one of the best approaches to spiritual warfare is to be strong in the Lord. We cannot stand victoriously against Satan's attacks in our own power. All of our help comes from the Lord. We must stand in the power of God's might and effectively use His armor. What is God's armor and how can the use of them effectively prepare us for spiritual warfare?

What are the components of God's armor?

Clinton Arnold said, "The powerful and evil emissaries of the devil need to be resisted with the powerful armor of God" (Arnold 1989, 68). The biblical framework emphasizes that the child of God must put on the whole armor of God. The full armor includes the belt of truth, the breastplate of righteousness, the sandals of peace, the shield of faith, the helmet of salvation, and the sword of the spirit, His Word. Paul in the book of Ephesians declares that the "Sword of the Spirit" is the only weapon of offense in this list of armor (Eph 6: Application, 2541). We can resist the devil's schemes by putting on the armor of God. Listed below are a detailed description of the elements of God's armor and the affirming key scriptures taken from an article titled "Ministries Spiritual Warfare" www.letusreason.org.

The Elements of God's Armor

- The Belt of Truth - An attitude of honesty and integrity, truth, which is the word and Jesus, is our foundation. Everything a Christian does is based on truth which is the word and our lives. The enemy cannot move us into his ways if we walk in truth.

- The Breastplate of Righteousness - Our protective gear. This protects our vital organs. Satan attacks this area often by condemning us for not being righteous.

- The Sandals of Peace - Feet that are ready to go and take the gospel of peace - speaks of servanthood to our Lord Jesus Christ.

- The Shield of Faith - our protection from the fiery darts (flaming arrows) of the enemy... Trusting in Christ--knowing that He is with us interceding on our behalf.

- The Helmet of Salvation - Knowing where we came from and where we are going, a guarded future. It is to protect our minds with knowing we are in Him and in the faith.

- The Sword of the Spirit - Our defensive weapon to win in the battles...The word which can cut and expose everything (Heb. 4:12) will do its ministry in Christian lives if we use it skillfully and in faith.

- Praying for Everyone - Watch and pray lest you enter temptation, prayerlessness is powerlessness. It is the quick road to defeat. Christians must be in the attitude of prayer.

Affirming Key Scriptures

1. Christians should put on the whole armor each day (Eph. 6:11-18). This is done by reading the word and knowing Christ and applying His teachings. When we stand in Christ, we are victorious.

2. Be sober and vigilant against Satan and his wiles (2 Pet. 5:8-9). Be aware of his attacks as well as distractions.

3. Give Satan no place (Eph. 4:27; Jam. 4:7). Fight his temptations as soon as they are discovered in thought.

4. Christians overcome Satan by standing on the word of God and in the Spirit power who strengthens our weaknesses (Matt. 1:11; Jn. 2:14).

5. We overcome Satan also by the blood of Jesus and our testimony (Rev. 12:11). We cannot be removed if we hold onto Christ by faith.

6. Believers overcome Satan in the name of Jesus Christ and his merits (Eph. 2:20-22).

7. Watch and pray that you do not enter into temptation (Matt. 26:41; Matt. 6:13). We are to circumspectly know the evil around us that can influence and affect our spiritual life.

Our life in Christ begins with learning, affirming, and trusting in each part of the armor of God in spiritual warfare. We have the authority and the strength to resist Satan's temptations, by submitting to God, standing in Christ, and putting on His armor (www.letusreason. org, 2006, 11). Paul concludes his list of armor with the admonishing us to pray unselfishly. To stand against the wiles of the devil we must also pray before, during, and after spiritual warfare.

What role does prayer play in fighting Satan?

According to Arnold, Prayer is an essential spiritual weapon. He said, "Pray for inner strengthening through the Holy Spirit and the indwelling Christ who roots the life of a believer in love and for a personal knowledge of power and love of God" (Arnold 1989, 86). Prayer is the language of faith, feeling, and love. Prayer is communion with God. Prayer positions us to be in fellowship with the Lord. Prayer is an intercession between Christians and God, an intimate two-way conversation. Christian prayer requires attentiveness and the readiness through active and watchful waiting to hear, receive, and cooperate in what God imparts. In times of stress and difficulty, we can call on the Lord in prayer. When we are confronted by Satan we must pray. When we are tempted by Satan, we must pray. To stand against the wiles of the devil, we must pray. When we are under satanic attack, we must pray. We must utilize the privilege of prayer and discover the power of prayer in fighting Satan. The power comes when we simply open up our heart and talk to God.

Prayer is a powerful tool against satanic attack. Prayer is utilized as a weapon to penetrate strongholds that cannot be reached in any other way. Prayer is essential in the Christian life. Without it, our witness will be less effective, and we will be more vulnerable to the enemy. When we place our faith in God and lift our petitions before Him, Jesus makes the connection possible. It is our connection with God that equips us for spiritual warfare.

The power of prayer in fighting Satan has its real sources in Christ Jesus. He is our High Priest. The writer of Hebrews encourages us to come boldly to God's throne to find help and grace in the time of need (Heb. 4:14-16). The redemption that is in Jesus is total, involving every aspect of the person-body, soul, will, mind, emotions, and spirit. With Him we have the potential to become more and more like Jesus and less likely to be deceived by Satan.

The Holy Spirit is also the source of power in our prayers. "In Ephesians 6:18-20 prayer is seen as essential to the army of believers with the power of God in order to resist the diabolic powers who would seek to prevent them from living according to Christian ethics" (Arnold 1989, 112). The Holy Spirit is a divine resource given by Jesus, sent from the Father to every Christian to help us stand in victory over intercedes on our behalf. The Apostle Paul said,

> Likewise, the Spirit helps us in our weakness: for we do not know how to pray as we ought, but that very Spirit intercedes with signs too deep for words. And God, who searches the heart, knows what is the mind of the Spirit, because the Spirit intercedes for the saints according to the will of God. (Rom. 8:26-27NRSV)

We must resist the temptation to assume that we may rely only on our own strength. It is only when we approach God's throne in prayer, in the power of the Holy Spirit, with faith believing God will give us power, that we can stand strong against the strategies and plan of Satan.

While preparing this project, the literature reviewed confirmed what I had been taught and experienced. The Bible is full of examples of the power of prayer. Stephen, a man full of faith and power, was stoned to death by religious leaders. Before he died, the Holy Spirit empowered him to speak up and stand up against the attack and pray for his accusers (Acts 7:54-60). When Paul and Silas were imprisoned in a Philippi jail, they prayed and God delivered them (Acts 16:16-24). Jesus prayed in the garden of Gethsemane, and His father gave Him the strength to resist the devil and complete his assignment, the pan of salvation (Luke 22:39-46).

There is power in prayer! The Apostle Paul said, "Do not be anxious about anything, but in everything, by prayer and petition, with thanksgiving, present your requests to God. The peace of God, which transcends all understanding, will guard your hearts and minds in Jesus Christ" (Phil. 4:6-7).

To experience the power in prayer, we must rely thoroughly on God and have the faith to believe that with God we are more than conquerors.

CURRENT MODELS AND PRACTICES

What are the books and articles saying about spiritual warfare? How can the information assist in our understanding of spiritual warfare and the identification and use of God's armor? What is God's armor and how can the use of them effectively prepare us for spiritual warfare?

In order to be effective in our efforts through a six-week course to equip participants to understand spiritual warfare as well as their identification of and use of God's armor I researched several models. The current models of *Charles Kraft with Mark White* (2000) *Behind Enemy Lines,* Tony Evans (1998) *The Battle is the Lord's,* and Edward Murphy (1996) *The Handbook of Spiritual Warfare* are just a few that opened my understanding of today's theological framework. Each author offered in their books various models that supported this project and comprehensively explained key issues.

Spiritual warfare is a struggle between good and evil. It can also be seen as a battle between right and wrong. Spiritual warfare refers to the believer's multidimensional war affecting personal behavior in the battle against Satan and his fallen angels. In his book, *The Battle is the Lord,* Tony Evans defines spiritual warfare as,

Conflict being waged in the invisible, spiritual realm that is being manifest in the visible, physical realm... spiritual warfare or conflict is a battle between invisible, angelic forces that affect you and me. The cause of the war is something you and I cannot see. But the effects are very visible in the kinds of problems... in day-to-day issues you face all of the time. (Evans 1998, 19)

I concur with the Tony Evans model. He said, "Spiritual warfare is that conflict being waged in the invisible, spiritual realm that is being manifest in the visible, physical realm" (Evans 1998, 19). Spiritual warfare is a battle between invisible, angelic forces that affects all human beings. Paul Hiebert, professor of Mission and Anthropology at Trinity Evangelical Divinity School in Deerfield, Illinois shares that the battle between good and evil is found in all religions.

Similar to Tony Evans, Paul Hiebert's defines spiritual warfare as the battle between good and evil. He continues his definition by disclosing that the conflict is experienced in every faucet of religions. He said:

> Battles between good and evil and of power encounters between good gods and evil demons are found in all religions. In Hinduism Rama battles Ravana, in Buddhism Buddha fights Mara, in Islam Allah wars against Shaitan, and in traditional religions tribal gods fight one another for conquest. (Hiebert 2006, 1)

Spiritual warfare shines a spotlight of truth on the basic problem of human existence and human history. Paul Hiebert's research reveals that,

> For most tribal people, ancestors, earthly spirits, witchcraft, and magic are very real. The people see the earth and sky as full of beings (gods, earthly divinities, ancestors, ghosts, evil shades, humans, animals, and nature spirits) that relate, deceive, bully, and battle one another for power and personal gain. These beings are neither totally good nor totally evil. They help those who serve or placate them. They harm those who oppose their wishes or who neglect them or refuse to honor them. Humans must placate them to avoid terrible disasters. (Hiebert 2006, 2)

People throughout history have argued the existence of spiritual warfare or have limited their understanding to what the Bible states in a historical context. There are Christians who believe every difficulty encountered in their life is a matter of spiritual warfare. However, there are others who would agree with the conflict but have not labeled the battle, spiritual warfare. My research unfolded the understanding of spiritual warfare of Harvey Cox, theologian from Harvard University which could possibly support this hypothesis.

Harvey Cox is against the use of the term *spiritual warfare*. He believes the following:

> When we talk about spiritual warfare, however, we are not envisioning armed conflict or the provocation of hostilities among people. We are taking the adjective spiritual quite seriously. We are suggesting that life is not just biology; there is a uniquely spiritual dimension to reality. There are unseen personal forces that have an impact on day-to-day life. Not all of these spirits are positive and benevolent either. There are many that are evil and bent on destruction. The Bible calls Christians to be aware of this and to prepare for a struggle. The biblical metaphor of spiritual warfare, then, is a shorthand way of referring to our conflict with these spirit forces. They are perpetrators of untold evil in both the physical realm and the moral realm. The Bible describes these spirits as especially working to keep people from responding to the redemptive message of the Lord Jesus Christ and to bring about the demise of the people of God. The gospel of deliverance we bring to people is actually a message of peace and reconciliation. (Arnold 2003, 25)

Regardless of the term used to label the conflict, Satan is real, as well as the spiritual warfare. Evil spiritual forces often use indistinguishable influences to encourage behaviors in Christians that are contrary to God's will. Pride, lust, envy, anger, lying, and rage are goals that Satan sets in his interactions with Christians. I like the simple description of Satan and his strategies. Tony Evans' statement:

> Satan's battle strategy is simple. He is out to deceive us, to trick us into buying his lies and temptations. He's been at

his plan for countless years, and he's good at it. Paul even
said that Satan can disguise himself as an "angel of light" (2
Cor. 11:14). Satan wants us to think he is right, he wants
you to follow him and not God. And not only is Satan good
at what he does, he can give you a good time while he is
deceiving you. (Evans 1998, 32)

Regardless of the term used to label the conflict, the effects are evident in the adversity and challenges experienced in day-to-day life. Charles Kraft and Mark White state:

One of Satan's primary tactics to thwart God's plans is to
get God's people to disobey him or to neglect their
relationship with him. This the enemy does most effectively
through either keeping people ignorant of what God desires
(2 Cor. 4:4) or by deceiving them into disobeying (Gen.
3:1-7). (Kraft and White 2000, 47)

Theological perspectives indicate that Satan tries to enmesh his stronghold in the everyday lives of individuals and families. He uses subversive tactics to gain ground in the Church of Jesus Christ and erect strongholds that hinder the work of God. Evans states, "Bringing spiritual warfare inside the doors of the Church is a key strategy of the Devil. He knows if he can weaken the church internally, he can weaken its witness and impact on the world" (Evans 1998, 10). Charles Kraft and Mark White share a definition of spiritual warfare that is multidimensional. Satan can deceive the people of God; and lead them into disobeying God on both the ground and cosmic levels.

According to Kraft and White, ground-levels and cosmic-levels deal with most of the direct effects of demonic beings on humans, such as temptation to sin, demonic harassment, oppression, and demonization (demons inhabiting people) (Kraft with White 2000, 66). Both Kraft and White continue,

The sin problem has three major dimensions. First of all,
sin is personal; it comes from within as we engage in
warfare with the flesh. Secondly, sin is social; it comes
from without as we engage in warfare with the world

> around us. And thirdly, sin is supernatural; it comes from above as we engage in warfare with Satan's invisible cosmic kingdom of evil made up of Satan himself and all the demonic hierarchy under his command (Eph. 6:10-20). I call this third area "evil supernaturalism." It is the main focus of ground-level spiritual warfare. (Kraft and White, 2000, 65-66)

Kraft and White argue that all Christians are tempted to sin and the enemy we face is an invisible enemy. The battles we face between good and evil are unavoidable. The conflict we face cannot be won with our limited power. What is the current model used to equip Christians for spiritual warfare? How can we stand strong against a willful, coordinated assault of Satan?

To equip Christians for spiritual warfare, it is imperative to remain open for the guidance of the Holy Spirit, who speaks to the inner being and provides guidance as to the right things to do. Those who listen and follow this spiritual path will remain under the guiding control and protection of the Holy Spirit. The indwelling power of the Holy Spirit can actively transform us into the image of Christ and give us the needed strength to stand against satanic attack.

In the Harper's Study Bible, P. J. Achtemeier suggests that we rely on the power of the Holy Spirit. The Holy Spirit is our source of inspiration and power. He is the vehicle of God's revelation and activity who gives the Christian their wisdom, courage, and power as gifts resulting from the possession of the Holy Spirit. "The Spirit makes Christians one 'in Christ' and empowers them, not only for the mission of the church, but also for the moral and ethical life appropriate to those who understand themselves to be people of the new age" (Achtemeier 1985, 401). We must rely on the presence of God to get through the tough times, the temptations and the distractions that come from Satan and his demonic attack. The spiritual disciplines are also a current model and practice to equip Christians for spiritual warfare according to Terry Wardle.

The biblical framework emphasizes that Christians practice the spiritual disciplines to position the believer to become spiritual. The only way to stay in the realm of the spirit is to practice spiritual disciplines.

"Nothing is more important to your life than developing intimacy with God and communing with Him" (Wardle 2004, 26). To seek Him intimately, love Him passionately, experience spiritual intimacy positions us to hear His voice. Greater intimacy with God will increase our spiritual maturity and nurture personal holiness in our lives. Wardle suggests as Christians we must, "Silence the noise of your troubled thoughts and burdened emotions, enter His presence by the Spirit, and offer the sacrifice of praise He deserves" (Wardle 2004, 196). There in the presence of God we will find that God will meet us in our weakness.

Prayer is a spiritual discipline that is vital to the life of the Christian and the first great rule is that we maintain a general discipline in his/her life. Believers need to pray for the ability to endure the stress of trials, the boldness to challenge immorality and heresy, the power to enter conflict, and the stamina not to grow weary. These shall be wrapped in the gift of love, since Christians cannot wage war against sin successfully unless there is also love for the sinner. Leanne Payne asserts:

We will be looking to no other power, no other intervention but Him. This looking straight to God and receiving His battle plan keeps us on a safe ground in another very important matter-we know that we are to hate sin, but we are not to hate our enemy. (Payne 2004, 185)

The congregation at Unity Baptist Church has been taught that Satan's attacks are personal, often involving hearts, emotions, and faith. Spending time with God will help improve and enhance our efforts to stand victoriously against the wiles of the devil. It is my prayer that, with the help of the Holy Spirit, all Christians will be able to grow in faith and develop a closer relationship with God. An intimate relationship with Him and an understanding of spiritual warfare will lead Christians to experience joy as well as realize the need for the armor of God. It is my prayer that, with the help of the Holy Spirit, all Christians will be able to grow in faith and develop a closer relationship with God. An intimate relationship with Him and an understanding of spiritual warfare will lead Christians to experience joy as well as realize the need for the armor of God.

I like Dr. Charles Stanley's current method for equipping Christians for spiritual warfare. Dr. Charles Stanley, Pastor of First Baptist Church, Atlanta, Georgia said, "These weapons of our warfare are especially important, I believe, in the heat of a temptation" (Stanley 2004, 159). To withstand these attacks, Christians must rely on God's strength and equip themselves with the full armor of God. Apostle Peter states, "In the Christian life, we battle against rulers and authorities, the powerful evil forces of fallen angels headed by Satan, who is a vicious fighter" (1 Pet. 5:8). Both the theological and biblical approach to this project confirms that participants in this project understand, as well as identify and use the full armor of God.

APPLICATIONS IN THE CONTEXT

I have discovered that the research literature has affirmed the need for additional resources and opportunities of study in the areas of spiritual warfare and the armor of God because the Christian life is a conflict. Every person born into this world enters into a conflict between good and evil. Often, the arena for spiritual battle is fought within the human mind. Many Christians today are ill- prepared for spiritual conflict, and there is nothing in the world that can arm the church for spiritual victory. Our adversary is real. Satan is crafty, deceitful, and tricky. Satan and his host are committed to hinder and obstruct the work of Christ. The forces of evil are powerful, numerous, and organized. Pastors, preachers, and teachers warn us not to fight the devil in our own power. We must acknowledge that our personal strength is limited.

Christians actively pursue spiritual discipline to be stronger and better prepared to resist Satan when faced with harassment by his hosts. The spiritual disciplines such as study, prayer, fasting, meditation, journaling, solitude, and worship position us to experience the power and presence of God in our lives. When we make ourselves available to Him and place ourselves before God, He can transform us and equip us with the resources for spiritual warfare. The project focused on participants understanding the nature of spiritual warfare and equipping Christian individuals with God's armor. This project focused on the impact of a six-week course taught at the Unity Baptist Church. The aim was to introduce scripture and literature that would be particularly meaningful to the participants and to determine the efficacy of spiritual warfare during a reflective six-week course.

The authors' personal faith has grown to dimensions that could not be imagined when this program started. I thank God for giving me power when I felt weak with no strength left to face temptation or to endure hardship in my life.

Christians should have very little problem conceptualizing life as a journey of transformation. Knowing God along the way is critically important to the process of spiritual warfare and spiritual guidance.

CHAPTER FOUR

METHODOLOGY

The purpose of this project was to measure the impact of a six-week course at Unity Baptist Church in Detroit, Michigan on the participants' understanding of spiritual warfare as well as their identification of and use of God's armor. The research question was: What is the impact of a six-week course at Unity Baptist Church in Detroit, Michigan in equipping participants to understand spiritual warfare and to identify and effectively use God's armor?

This project focused on increasing the understanding of spiritual warfare and equipping these Christian individuals with spiritual armor in preparation for inevitable encounters with the forces of darkness. The process included the introduction of scriptures that were particularly meaningful, as well as methods to determine the efficacy of spiritual warfare during a reflective six-week course.

This project explored concepts such as "spiritual warfare" and "equipping." To accomplish the purpose of this project, participants were encouraged to pray regularly. Participants were also engaged in exploring the theological, historical, contemporary understanding of spiritual warfare and the equipping power which comes from the presence of God's Holy Spirit.

Group members experienced the wisdom and power of God through their participation in scripture readings, study time, prayer, face-to-face communication, and meditation. The group met at Unity Baptist Church 6:00 - 8:00 pm each week for a period of six weeks. During that time, group members increased their understanding of spiritual warfare, learned different types of prayers and came to recognize the full armor (weapons) of God. They became aware of the cunning activities initiated by Satan and his demons such as promoting lies, idolatry, slander, and cults. They learned how to brace themselves for the inevitable spiritual warfare. During the six-week course, we prayed and rededicated our lives to Christ. We found comfort in knowing that the spiritual armor of God is mighty and available for our defense against Satan.

CONTEXT

The class project was conducted at Unity Baptist Church in Detroit, Michigan. Unity Baptist Church was organized in December 1926 from a home- to-home prayer meeting and Bible study group of eight God-fearing African- American Christians who resided on the west side of Detroit. On March 17, 1963, Reverend Valmon D. Stotts was called to the pastorate of Unity Baptist Church. He motivated the congregation towards faith in God and his vision of a larger and more spacious church facility in order to accommodate the rapid membership growth. The congregation grew numerically and spiritually. According to the scriptures, a pastor is given as a gift to the church to perfect, equip, and build up the body of Christ so that the church would experience unity and maturity in Christ. The Apostle Paul said,

> "It was he who gave some to be apostles, some to be prophets, some to be evangelists, and some to be pastors and teachers, to prepare God's people for works of service, so that the body of Christ may be built up until we all reach unity in the faith and in the knowledge of the Son of God and become mature, attaining to the whole measure of the fullness of Christ...." (Eph. 4:11-12)

Pastor Stotts is truly a gift from God, preaching and teaching our church to follow the example of Christ and to grow to be more like Him.

Teaching is one of the most important strategies for Unity Baptist Church to foster spiritual growth. Pastor Stotts established a Christian Education (CE) program which has become a bridge to connect all educational ministries in order to serve its membership and community in an orderly manner. "Everything should be done in a fitting and orderly way" (1 Cor. 14:4). The CE program structure places every ministry under the guidance of the pastor and the Board of Christian Education. The new CE plan provides the opportunity for more of the church family to participate in the study of God's Word.

In its 82 years of existence, the membership of Unity Baptist Church has grown to approximately 3,000. Members in this large congregation are predominantly black, middle-class people. Many of them work as teachers, nurses, lawyers, doctors, police officers, preachers, and factory workers. There are also a number of retirees and young people. The Church has two regular services on Sunday morning at 8:00 and 11:00, with a specialized service for children in a separate area of the Church during the 11:00 worship. Teaching and preaching in the name of Jesus, are yet two of the most important ministries in the church of which they experience numerical and spiritual growth.

The Church continues to spread the Good News of the Gospel through its formal and informal educational programs. The truths of the Scriptures are presented clearly, and individuals may respond by personal faith in Jesus Christ and grow toward spiritual maturity. "And how from infancy you have known the Holy Scriptures, which are able to make you wise for salvation through faith in Christ Jesus" (2 Timothy 3:15).

PARTICIPANTS

The participants in this project were all members of the Unity Baptist Church. They were not required to have any specific religion, education or skill level, or knowledge on spiritual warfare. The only requirement was their interest in the subject and their willingness to commit to participate in the course. The ages of the participants ranged between 19 and 60 years. Participants were all African Americans. Their educational levels ranged from high graduate, college students and college graduates.

PROCEDURE

The project was designed to help participants understand spiritual warfare and equip them to identify and effectively use God's armor. The overall purpose of this project was to measure the impact of a six-week course at Unity Baptist Church in Detroit, Michigan on the participants' understanding of spiritual warfare as well as their identification of and use of God's armor. The project involved first gathering and selecting the appropriate material for the six-week course and then devising a strategy for assessing its effectiveness. The procedure for accomplishing this project was as follows:

- I selected and analyzed literature pertaining to various theological concepts i.e., the Holy Spirit, spiritual disciplines, spiritual warfare, Satan and demons, the armor of God, and the equipping of the saints.

- I developed a pre-test survey to determine the participants understanding of spiritual warfare and the armor of God. A post-test was developed to determine the impact and effectiveness of the projected goals.

- I analyzed the data and prepared it for presentation in this document. The results will be presented in Chapter 5.

The sessions were held at the Unity Baptist Church for two hours per week. The sessions began with worship, scripture readings, prayer and meditation. Opening prayer was used to invite the Lord, in the presence of the Holy Spirit. The Word of God was read to help the participants' minister to each other. These spiritual disciplines were very effective in preparing the hearts and minds for study and to seek an understanding of the prepared lessons.

Following our devotional period, ten to fifteen minutes was designated to study and discussion. Meaningful scripture readings as well as study guides and methods were used to facilitate discussion, meditation, and prayer. Materials used included handouts, computer with online access, blackboard, CD player, and inspirational music. At the conclusion of the class, assignments were given for the next session. After the closing prayer a period meditation and reflection followed with participants exiting at will. This procedure was the standard format used in every session. The following topics were covered during the time designed for study and discussion.

- *What* is *Spiritual Warfare?*
- *Are Lucifer and Satan the Same Being?*
- God's *Kingdom of Light* versus *Satan's Kingdom of*

Darkness.
- *The doctrine of the Holy Spirit.*
- *Christian Strategies for Spiritual Warfare.*
- *The Armor of God.*
- *The Model of Jesus*
- *The benefits of Spiritual Disciplines in spiritual warfare*

The responses and comments from the participants were taken into consideration to determine the effectiveness of the course. Special attention was given to the possibilities for its improvement and the possibilities to present the course at other churches within the community.

ASSESSMENT

The major goal of the project was to have participants engage in exploring the realms of spiritual warfare. The project was designed to measure the impact of a six-week course on understanding spiritual warfare and to equip participants to identify as well as and effectively use God's resources. This was determined by the assessment of participants using a survey of spirituality in the form of a pre-test and post-test developed by the author. The assessment tools I developed used a rating scale of 1 - 5 to determine the group effectiveness, with 5 being strongly agree and 1, being strongly disagree. Both surveys contained identical closed-ended questions with space for additional comments.

The assessment tool was called "Spiritual Warfare Survey" (see Appendix 2). It measured the group's understanding about spiritual warfare. This survey was based on an ordinal scale with a five-scale range:

5	=	Strongly Agree
4	=	Agree
3	=	Neither Agree Nor Disagree
2	=	Disagree
1	=	Strongly Disagree

The requested answers on this scale ranked the progression of agreement to disagreement of the participants understanding of spiritual warfare and the resources God provides for victory against satanic attacks. A neutral rank of neither agree nor disagree was used for statements for which the participants had neutral beliefs.

The responses and comments from the participants were taken into consideration to determine the effectiveness of the six-week course, possibilities for its improvement, and opportunities for additional classes.

Chapter five will report the results of this study, including the goals of this project, and will also support data for the six-week course on Spiritual Warfare.

CHAPTER FIVE

PROJECT OUTCOMES

This project focused on the Christian individual's understanding of spiritual warfare as well as the identification and use of God's armor. The purpose of this chapter is to report the results of the study. Survey results will provide the data to support the content and format of the study and its effectiveness in equipping the participants for satanic attack. Further, it will provide strong support for the need to change. I will make observations from the goals of the study, show the supporting data and interpret the data.

This chapter presents the major results relevant to each of the working project goals. The goals were as follows:

- Participants will incorporate the concepts of the armor (weapons) of God in their faith walk.
- Participants will gain an awareness of Satan's attacks in their lives.
- Participants will gain an enhanced knowledge of scriptura l examples that support the significance of putting on the whole armor of God.
- Participants will deepen their awareness of the work of the Holy Spirit in victory over the forces of darkness.
- Participants will demonstrate their understanding of spiritual warfare and God's armor.
- Participants will practice putting on the full armor of God.
- Participants will exercise trust in the Holy Spirit to empower them against the forces of darkness.

The participants were given a pre-test survey before the course began and a post-test survey after the completion of the course to measure the impact of the six-week class. The assessment tool titled "the Spiritual Warfare Survey" was designed to determine the participants' level of understanding of spiritual warfare. The survey was also designed to measure the participants' knowledge, as well as use of the resources God provides Christians to battle the forces of evil (Appendix 2). A pre-test survey was given to the nine participants in the course at the beginning of the first class.

FINDING RELATED TO PROJECT GOALS

This section reports the synthesized data from the pre-test survey. The survey asked the participants to answer twelve questions to determine their level of understanding of spiritual warfare and the armor of God.

The goals were prioritized according to their findings to best increase differences between the average pre-test scores and average post-test scores of all the participants. The statements listed below each goal were the actual pre-test statements with the corresponding number (Appendix 2).

Goals Two and Five

Participants will gain an awareness of Satan's attacks in their lives. Participants will demonstrate their understanding of spiritual warfare and God's armor.

Goals Two and Five of this project were to assist participants in their understanding of spiritual warfare. It was also my desire to question their knowledge of the doctrine of Satan and Demonology and his method of attack. Goals, two and five were also designed to question their awareness of assured victory against Satan. God has already defeated Satan! To assess these goals, participants rated the eight following statements:

- Spiritual warfare is defined as the invisible confrontation between the forces of God and the forces of the devil.
- Scripture clearly confirms that Satan is the foe of every human being.

- Fallen angels alert us to the way that Christians can be tempted.
- Spiritual warfare is a proactive approach to the Christians' faith.
- The angel Lucifer became ambitious to be equal with God.
- God cast Satan and his followers (1/3) of the angels) out of Heaven.
- Demons are believed to be real.
- God has already defeated Satan.

Table 1 on the next page shows data obtained from replies to these statements.

Participants used the Likert Scale's five-point rating in which 5 = Strongly Agree; 4 = Agree; 3 = Neither Agree Nor Disagree; 2 = Disagree; and 1 = Strongly Disagree.

The statistic measure used was determined by overall average of the response to each statement of the Likert Scale. Pre-test and post-test average scores were given and a post-test average score was given. The differences of the pre-and post-test average scores show an increase of participants' awareness.

In the first assessment under Goals Two and Five, statements 11 and 12 were supported by the participants' knowledge and understanding of spiritual warfare. The participants' pre-test average score increased from 4.77 to a post-test average score of 5.0. Participants studied the Biblical views of spiritual warfare. Afterwards they were able to give testimonies of spiritual warfare (conflict) in the Church, their personal lives and in their communities.

Table 1. Reported understanding spiritual warfare and the doctrine of Satan (Goals Two and Five)

Item Content (#)	Pre-test Average	Post-test Average	Increased Scores
Spiritual warfare is defined as the invisible confrontation between the forces of God and the forces of the devil. (statement 1)	4.77	5.0	+23%
Scripture clearly confirms that Satan is the foe of every human being. (statement 2)	4.66	5.0	+22%
Fallen angels alert us to the way that Christians can be tempted. (statement 4)	3.33	4.88	+80%
Spiritual warfare is a proactive approach to the Christians' faith. (statement 7)	4.22	4.66	+44%
The angel Lucifer became ambitious to be equal with God. (statement 9)	4.66	4.66	0%
God cast Satan and his followers (1/3) of the angels) out of Heaven. (statement 10)	4.44	5.0	+56%
Demons are believed to be real. (statement 11)	4.77	5.0	+23%
God has already defeated Satan. (statement 12)	4.77	4.77	0%

Note: Nine Participants provided answers to these statements.

In the second assessment under Goals Two and Five, statements 2 and 11, showed participants felt the scriptures confirmed the existence of Satan. Satan the tempter is real and is the enemy of the church. Biblical records also confirmed that Satan was thrown from Heaven and defeated by God. The data from these statements proved that the participants' pre-test average scores increased from 4.66 to a post-test average score of 5.0. Participants found the study of Paul's letter to the Ephesians very helpful. Ephesians 6:10-18, reminds us that Satan is the ruler of darkness. Satan leads the evil and powerful forces of fallen angels in a constant battle to defeat God's people. Spiritual warfare is conflict of which every Christian will encounter.

In the third assessment under Goals Two and Five, to my amazement, statement 9 showed no increase in the participants' knowledge of Satan's desire to be equal with God. These statements show that both the pre-and post-test average score was 4.66. It was great to see that the nine participants believed that God has already defeated Satan. However, data did not support an increase in their understanding that the battle was already won. Both the pre- and post-test average scores remained 4.77. I was surprised to see the major changes in the participants' response to statements four and ten. Data would suggest that the participants' understanding of Satan's fall from increased from 4.44 to a post- test average score of 5.0 an increase of 56%. The greatest increase in their understanding of the goal was in the area of the Christian temptation. Data suggests that participants' understanding of how fallen angels alert us to the possibility of temptation pre-test average score 3.33 increased to 4.88, an increase of 80%. This increase showed a substantial change in the participants' knowledge of spiritual warfare through the witness of fallen angels. The participants learned the reality of the challenges and temptations all Christians will endure.

Overall, the participants were enlightened with a greater understanding of spiritual warfare. They recognized that spiritual warfare has an impact on the lives of all Christians. The participants also reported having a deeper knowledge of Satan and his demonic attacks. They studied how to discern and recognize the attacks of Satan in their lives. Moreover, the participants are more comfortable with the subject and as supported by the statistical findings of this study, are much less likely to avoid the issue. Data reported that the participants were in total agreement that the increase in knowledge of spiritual warfare had a positive effect on their spiritual lives.

Goals One, Three and Six

Participants will incorporate the concepts of the armor (weapons) of God in their faith walk.

Participants will gain an enhanced knowledge of scriptural examples that support the significance of putting on the whole armor of God.

Participants will practice putting on the full armor of God.

The aim of Goals One, Three and Six was to help participants identify as well as effectively use the full armor of God. To assess these goals, participants rated the three following statements:

1. Ephesians 6: 11 instructs Christians to put on the full armor of God in order to take a stand against the devil's schemes.
2. God's Word, presented to us through Scripture is trustworthy.
3. Prayer is utilized as a weapon to penetrate strongholds.

Participants used the Likert Scale's five-point rating in which 5= Strongly Agree; 4 = Agree; 3 = Neither Agree Nor Disagree; 2 = Disagree; and 1 = Strongly Disagree. The statistic measure used was determined by overall average of the response to each statement of the Likert Scale. A pre-test average score was given and a post-test average score was given. The differences between the pre-and post-test showed the average growth increase.

Table 2 presents the data relevant to Goals One, Three and Six.

Table 2. Participants learned the concepts of the full armor (weapons) of God.

Item Content (#)	Pre-test Average	Post-test Average	Increased Scores
Ephesians 6:11 instructs Christians to put on the full armor of God in order to take a stand against the devil's schemes. (statement 6)	5.0	5.0	0%
God's word, presented to us through Scripture is trustworthy. (statement 3)	5.0	5.0	0%
Prayer is utilized as a weapon to penetrate strongholds. (statement 5)	4.77	4.88	+11%

Note: Nine Participants provided answers to this question.

In the first assessment under Goals One, Three, and Six, data for statements three and six propose no increase in the participants' understanding of the full armor of God. The participant's pre-and post-test average scores for both statements registered 5.0, the highest scores possible. This high score means that the participants already fully understood these concepts or perhaps the course served to confirm their understanding.

In the second assessment under Goals One, Three, and Six, statement five data showed little increase in the participants' knowledge that prayer can be used as a weapon against evil strongholds. This statement showed that the participants' pre-test average score increased from 4.77 to a post-test average score of 4.88.

Overall, the participants reported an overwhelming confidence in the reliability of God's Word. They also learned the concepts of the full armor of God. The participants recognized the necessity of wearing the full armor of God in order to stand against the devil's trickery, deceitfulness, and demonic strategies. The participants reflected on prayer as an essential component of God's armor. They understood that protective armor is strengthened through daily prayer, which builds a greater intimacy with God. In response to prayer, the participants understood that God often sends angels to strengthen, encourage, and protect His people. The participants were able to experience a greater intimacy with God through prayer. The participants were able to identify the armor of God, as well as encouraged to 'put on' God's armor.

Goals Four and Seven

Participants will deepen their awareness of the work of the Holy Spirit in victory over the forces of darkness.

Participants will exercise trust in the Holy Spirit to empower them against the forces of darkness.

Table 3 presents the data relevant to Goals Four and Seven.

Table 3. Participants deepened their awareness of the Holy Spirit's ministry in Christians against Satan and the forces of darkness.

Item Content (#)	Pre-test Average Score	Post-test Average Scores	Increased Scores
Christians need divine help to deal with Satan's attacks. (statement 8)	4.8	4.8	0%

Note: Nine Participants provided answers to this question.

    In the first assessment under Goals Four and Seven, statement eight data showed no increase about deepening their understanding of the Holy Spirit's ministry in the life of the Christian. This statement showed that the participants' pre-and post-test average scores were the same 4.8. Although the average score did not change at the completion of the course, the participants were consistent in their opinion. The high score likely indicated that the participants' already had a deep understanding of the Holy Spirit's ministry in the life of the Christian.

    Overall, the participants acknowledged the need for divine resources to stand against satanic forces. The participants were firm in their conviction that spiritual strength and courage are necessary in spiritual warfare and they have no sufficient strength of their own. All of their sufficiency is derived from the indwelling power of the Holy Spirit. Participants were encouraged to "put on" the full armor of God and trust the Holy Spirit to empower them against the forces of darkness. This data suggests that while most participants felt they had the knowledge to identify and equip themselves with the armor of God, they were more prepared and willing to step into action to do so after participating in this research project. Thereby, the participants would be equipped for spiritual warfare. Their testimonies reinforced the validity of this research. A six-week course proved to be effective in equipping participants to understand spiritual warfare, as well as identify and use of God's armor.

    Chapter Six will offer some reflections on this dissertation project. It will offer some suggestions about the course content and other variables that could have affected the outcome of the results of this project. Chapter Six will also offer some steps toward further studies and applications for additional courses in the future on equipping Christians for spiritual warfare. Finally, it will provide me the time to reflect on the practical wisdom gleaned from this study, applications to ministry, and my personal goals and conclusions.

CHAPTER SIX

REFLECTIONS AND IMPLICATIONS

The purpose of this project was to measure the impact of a six-week course at Unity Baptist Church in Detroit, Michigan on the participants' understanding of spiritual warfare as well as their identification of and use of God's armor. The research question was: What is the impact of a six-week course at Unity Baptist Church in Detroit, Michigan in equipping participants to understand spiritual warfare and to identify and effectively use God's armor?

> Satan is very good at protecting himself from what he knows to be a power much greater than his. He knows that God has infinitely more power than he has and that Jesus passed this power on to us. Satan's primary strategy, therefore, is to keep God's people ignorant and deceived so that we cannot use God's power against him. (Kraft 2002, 25)

REFLECTIONS

When I reflect on the current work in this discipline, I know that this project is significant because many Christians in our churches are not equipped for spiritual warfare. Satan has and is currently seeking to destroy the faith of believers and deceiving and persuading them to turn from the one true God, to the gods of this world. From creation God has given individuals the opportunity to choose whose path to follow. Humans have freewill to decide for themselves if they want to belong to the Kingdom of Light or the Kingdom of Darkness. Jesus is the light of the world! Satan is of darkness. Christ makes it clear that there are two distinct and opposing spiritual kingdoms, God's Kingdom and the Kingdom of Satan. Each person must decide to which side he or she belongs: Christ's or Satan's. Many have chosen to follow Christ and have committed their lives daily to Him; however, there are many others who have chosen to follow Satan.

When I reflect on this particular challenge I ask, how can I best prepare God's people for battle with Satan when the warfare is inevitable? The attacks of Satan come in an array of forms, such as illness, envy, strife, and hatred. How can I equip believers to stand against the schemes of the devil? The concern of this project was to help participants understand spiritual warfare and equip them to stand and not fall by the wayside. Therefore, I selected and analyzed literature pertaining to various theological concepts i.e., spiritual warfare, Satan and demons, the armor of God, and the transforming and enabling power of the Holy Spirit. My ultimate goal was to help participants identify as well as use the resources God has provided. They need to know that God's righteousness can be worn as our breastplate to protect us from Satan's temptations.

When I reflect on the current work in this discipline and my personal educational experience, I have been exposed to many helpful concepts that will enhance my ministry. Preaching and teaching are the ministries of which I have been called. I learned that educational opportunities can be made available, yet many Christians will not take advantage of the opportunity. While my goals were to teach others, I also came away with a greater understanding of human nature and spirituality.

This project has enhanced my previous understanding of the reality of spiritual warfare and God's resources. This research reminded me that Satan is still deceitful, cunning, and intelligent. If he cannot trick you with his schemes in one manner, he will use another. There were times when I faced the temptations of Satan and endured hardship during my doctoral journey at Ashland Theological Seminary. However, I put on the full armor of God and experienced the strength of the Lord. I am grateful for the spiritual power He gave me in my weakest hours.

As a result, my personal faith has grown to dimensions I could not have imagined. I now, like others, firmly take the existence of Satan and his strategies even more seriously. My personal prayer and meditation positioned me to allow God's mysterious and silent presence within me to become the reality that gives meaning, shape, and purpose to everything I do. Meditation brought my distracted mind to stillness, silence, and attention. Making time for quiet moments of reflection supported my efforts to remain alert, yet humble to the works of the Holy Spirit in my life and ministry.

When I reflect on the condition of our society, I ask how I can help the fallen to experience the forgiving love of Christ. When I reflect on the sins of fallen clergy and the fact that we too have and can become entangled with the snares of the devil, I wonder how I can lead us through spiritual warfare and to victory over Satan. When I reflect on the many tensions initiated by Satan that Christians face, I want to be able to point them to the tools and resources God has provided. Thus, it is vital that we provide learning opportunities where our disciples can voice their doubts, anger, frustrations, fears, and disappointments with themselves. My passion is to help position them to move from confession of sin, to repentance, to forgiveness, to deliverance and celebration. Moreover, it is my desire to equip them with the armor of God in order to become victors and not victims. As believers, the integrity and credibility of our life and ministry requires us to walk the talk.

When I reflect on this project, I was amazed by the many Christians who approached me and inquired: "Spiritual warfare? What is it?" The participants also asked, "What is Satan?" I was even more astonished at the degree of commitment from the Unity Baptist Church members and their response to spiritual warfare. Although there were only nine members who participated in the course offered at Unity Church, there were many more that needed to understand spiritual warfare, and identify as well as use the armor of God.

This project provided me with the answers. What is Satan? Satan is an adversary of God. Satan is pure evil and one who loves warfare. He is deceitful and a liar. He creates chaos, strife, divisions, and fights. He attempts to frustrate and obstruct God's kingdom in every way. Satan uses cunning tricks and creates circumstances that target the inherent weaknesses of human beings. This project defined Satan and also gave me insight to several strategies that are important to our conflict with Satan and victory with Christ.

Understanding spiritual warfare is not enough. Since the battle is not of earthly origin, it cannot be won using carnal weapons. To stand courageously and victoriously against the devil's schemes we must be equipped with the full armor of God. We must also pray, place our faith and trust in God, and rely on the power of the Holy Spirit. These are resources God has provided us to overcome the devil's schemes.

APPLICATION

The first area of application was to schedule a meeting with Pastor Stotts and discuss the plan of teaching this class at Unity Baptist Church twice a year. I gave him the syllabus and several reasons why this class should be taught. First, Christians need to know the importance of understanding the doctrine of Satan and spiritual warfare. Second, in order for Christians to stand against satanic attacks, they must be taught to identify as well as to use the armor of God. Third, God has given every believer the gift of the Holy Spirit; however, some believers don't understand how the Holy Spirit empowers us to stand against the strategies of Satan. Fourth, it is important for the church to know that the weapon of praise is a powerful resource against spiritual warfare.

I also scheduled a meeting with then President of the Michigan Progressive Baptist Convention (MPBC), Rev. Dr. Sandra A. Fox, to discuss teaching this spiritual warfare class at our state convention throughout the year. The MPBC membership includes approximately 38 Baptist churches throughout Michigan. Teaching in the convention will provide an excellent opportunity to assist in equipping God's people for spiritual warfare.

I contacted Rev. Dr. Oscar King, then President of the Council of Baptist Pastors of Detroit and Vicinity, to request the opportunity to facilitate a four-week special lecture series on spiritual warfare. The Council membership includes both pastors and ministers. Because I am a member of the Council, I anticipate the opportunity to share my passion for equipping Christians for spiritual warfare. It may be a very enlightening experience for some pastors and ministers to become more aware of Satan's schemes. It is my desire that the class will help pastors and ministers know how they can effectively equip their congregations for spiritual warfare. Although the chance to teach the preachers will be challenging, I would be grateful for the opportunity to utilize the skills I have learned from this project.

The Metropolitan Sunday School Congress meets four times a year for a week. Churches across Michigan come together at this time to take Christian education classes. I planned to talk to the dean and request an opportunity to teach this spiritual warfare course.

The last area of application is to apply for a teaching position at Ashland Theological Seminary. Because of the information I have been taught by the professors at Ashland, and this project, I believe I will be an asset to the students at Ashland. This project has given me great insight into spiritual warfare, and I thank God for all I have learned. It is my desire and ultimate goal to equip as many Christians that I can, for spiritual warfare.

PERSONAL

Before starting the work on my Doctor of Ministry program, I was only vaguely aware of the seriousness of spiritual warfare. Often I ignored conversational references to spiritual warfare being at the root of adversity in someone's life. But now, after my research, I fully comprehend the reality of spiritual warfare and understand what we, as Christians, must know and do when we are under satanic attacks.

When I began this project, I was overwhelmed (devastated) as I became more aware of spiritual warfare and the effect it had on the children of God. The Lord stirred in me a passion to know where spiritual warfare originated. To my surprise, my research revealed spiritual warfare started in heaven or somewhere beyond the earth. At first, I could not believe what I had read, but soon realized its truth. Spiritual warfare is the struggle between good and evil. It is our battle with the spiritual unseen reality. The mission of Satan and his demons is to taunt, confuse, slander, harm, and destroy all humans.

Spiritual warfare became a reality to me through the Holy Spirit's ministry in my life. He created a hunger and thirst within me to seek an in-depth understanding of works of Satan. God chose to use me to help equip and prepare His people for spiritual warfare. Teaching Christians about spiritual warfare and methods of defense against such attacks is a part of the ministry of which I have been called.

My academic and theological pursuit at Ashland Theological Seminary (ATS) provided the opportunity to continue my journey to sharpen the gifts and tools God has provided and has worked through me. The experience has transformed my life and strengthened my relationship with God. I met and formed new relationships with others who were on the same journey. Moreover, I pray more and I am prepared to withstand Satan's attacks. I also desire to teach others about spiritual warfare My studies at ATS also assisted my understanding of doctrines of our faith, such as theology, demonology and the Ministry of the Holy Spirit. It was during my journey that God confirmed the biblical study of spiritual warfare as my area of concentration. The Spirit-led classes facilitated by ATS professors, suggested curriculum and special readings, and research prepared me academically for equipping Christians for spiritual warfare. The Holy Spirit guided my understanding, and He empowered me to effectively teach others about spiritual warfare.

Teaching the course on spiritual warfare at Unity Baptist Church in Detroit, Michigan for six weeks was a great experience for me, as well as for the participants in the class. The two-hour class sessions were so interesting that our conversations often continued for at least 20-to-30 minutes beyond the scheduled end time. It was an enlightening experience for everyone. Pastor Stotts of Unity Baptist Church stated that he would like me to teach this class every year. This invitation was extended as a result of this project.

I am grateful for the nine members of Unity Church who participated in the six-week course. Their commitment to the class was needed to measure the impact of the class; however, I know there are many others who yet need to be equipped for spiritual warfare.

My research for this project exposed me to what others have written about spiritual warfare. The knowledge I acquired from the many voices provided excellent resource for future classes. As I was teaching others what I had learned through my study, I too was confronted with satanic attacks. I taught others that God's people find themselves living frustrated and defeated lives, deceived, tricked and led astray by the devil. On this journey I experienced challenges initiated by the devil that left me feeling disappointed, frustrated, and at times overwhelming. Moreover, completing this project seemed difficult to overcome. Through this process, I depended on God's armor for protection. Even though we deal with the unseen, it does affect the Christian's life because we believe in God, Jesus, and the Holy Spirit. Satan would like to control our minds so we cannot discern the difference between good and evil. The devil attacked my mind and my health. The enemy was strong and the battle was real.

I began to feel faint and stopping for a while to stretch and catch my breath. In my weakened state, I prayed to God to help me complete this project. The pains in my chest continued, and I tried to ignore it. I stopped for a drink of water and later continued my writing. However, the pain in my chest continued. I heard the Spirit of God telling me to go to the doctor. Upon arrival, the doctor took a look at me and immediately hooked me up to an EKG machine. He told me if I had waited one more hour before coming to the hospital, I would have been *dead!* Thanks be to God! Since then, my health has improved, and there have been no other spiritual warfare attacks. This event solidified my belief and understanding that God's protective armor is the ultimate defense against Satan's interference in our lives.

This incident was an eye opener for me. Knowing the seriousness of the presence of satanic attacks and that, as Christians, we can war against satanic attacks if we are properly trained and equipped. God prepared me and gave me the victory. I pray and meditate on Him more. Sometimes I stay up late or get up early in the morning just to be in His presence. I am thankful for what God is doing in my life and the effect His influence has in my life and the lives of my family, friends, and others.

FURTHER STUDY

The need for further study is an undeniable compelling idea

because spiritual warfare is an integral part of the entire Christian experience. The Christian life is filled with constant spiritual battles. Satan continuously seeks whom he may devour and God's people still find themselves living frustrated and defeated lives led astray by the devil. One of the challenges for the church is how to prepare God's people with the resources to overcome the many obstacles Satan uses to trip up Christian people. He tricks many of us because we underestimate his power and/or ignore or fail to identify his activities in our day-to-day lives. Consequently, spiritual warfare deeply ingrains itself in our lives and we find his efforts difficult to discern or understand. We witness every day some of the means Satan uses as opportunities to lead our thoughts astray from a sincere and pure devotion to Christ.

The opportunity for further study is an undeniable compelling idea because prior to the six-week course, I discovered that many of the participants were unaware of the divine resources available to them to help them deal with the devil's attacks. They were firm in their conviction that spiritual strength and courage are necessary for spiritual warfare and that they have no sufficient strength of their own.

The specific purpose of this project was to measure the impact of a six week course at Unity Baptist Church in Detroit, Michigan on the participants' understanding of spiritual warfare as well as their identification of and use of God's armor. The six-week course addressed the need for Christians to understand Satan, his methods of attack, knowledge of God's resources, and how to effectively use them. Therefore, the areas of study would include a more in-depth research of the doctrines of Satan, spiritual warfare, the armor of God, and the ministry of the Holy Spirit.

The opportunity for further study is an undeniable compelling idea because spiritual warfare is not taught in many of our churches and "the devil made me do it" is more than a statement of the late Flip Wilson. Consequently, many believers are caught off guard by the inevitable spiritual warfare and have yielded to the temptation to sin. Moreover, they soon discover spiritual battles cannot be won by using earthly, carnal weapons. The Lord has provided His people everything they need to defeat the devil's efforts. Because Satan is tricky, demonic, deceptive, intelligent, and has the power to potentially hold even believers in bondage, the church must maintain its efforts to equip and empower God's people.

The opportunity for further study is a mandate for the church in order for God's people to understand the victory they have in Christ. Jesus became flesh, in the form of a man empowered by God, defeated Satan, died to pay the penalty for sin and to triumph over the devil. Jesus encourages us to put on the full armor of God. He invites us to fully bring ourselves before Him and pray sincerely from our hearts, sharing our own desires, feelings, experiences, and needs. He only asks that we be willing to trust God. We must teach God's people to invite Him into their lives and accept His protective covering of truth, faith, sword of the spirit, and salvation. This will be easier to achieve through formal instruction with guided discussion, prayer, and meditation.

This could raise the question about the research of this study and our efforts to suggest offering classes on "Spiritual Warfare" in our churches. It is the charge and responsibility of the local church to prepare God's people for spiritual conflict. The church universal must continue its efforts to equip the saints by offering classes and workshops. It is expedient that every believer is given the chance to understand spiritual warfare and how to use God's armor as a defense. We must strategically endeavor to create effective learning opportunities to educate and prepare Christians with the spiritual resources needed for spiritual warfare.

PERSONAL GOALS

The purpose of this project was to measure the impact of a six-week course at Unity Baptist Church in Detroit, Michigan on the participants' understanding of spiritual warfare as well as their identification of and use of God's armor. I have achieved all personal goals set for accomplishment by the completion of this project. They are as follows:

1. To increase personal awareness of spiritual warfare and its impact on daily life.

This project has helped the author to have an increased understanding of spiritual warfare and strengthened his Christian disciplines in the area of prayer, Bible study, and meditation.

2. To be better prepared to equip Christians for spiritual warfare.
   After six weeks of study regarding spiritual warfare, the author is truly inspired to tell others about God and His angelic kingdom and the confrontation with Satan and his demonic kingdom. The author will continue to instruct Christians about putting on the full armor of God.

3. To realize personal growth from developing and being a part of this spiritual experience.
   The author has grown in faith and commitment to the profession. He has a personal relationship with God, and will continue to experience a healthier and more profound relationship with Him.

4. To have a deeper personal relationship with God through Jesus Christ and the Holy Spirit.
   The author feels spiritually stronger, and he prays that the Holy Spirit will always be there to be his guide. He will continue to read the Holy Bible. As 2 Tim. 3: 16-17 states, "All scripture is God-breathed and is useful for teaching, rebuking, correcting, and training in righteousness, so that the man of God may be thoroughly equipped for every good work."

5. Through the administration of a pre-test and a post-test, participants demonstrated increased knowledge of spiritual warfare and the ability to identify and equip themselves with the armor of God.
   The results of the tests administered to the participants confirm increased knowledge of spiritual warfare and the ability and willingness of participants to use that knowledge daily in their spiritual lives.

CONCLUSION

This coursework has given me a new understanding on spiritual warfare. It has equipped and empowered me to be more effective in reaching out to equip Christians for spiritual warfare. This project has renewed my faith in God. Because I have grown spiritually, I have the confidence to teach others. With God on my side, I can recognize satanic attacks. I know with assurance that when I trust God and use the resources He has provided; I am equipped for spiritual warfare. My hope and prayer is for all Christians to become aware of the effect of spiritual warfare and the resources the full armor of God provides. My hope and prayer is for God to use me for His glory to help Christian identify as well as effectively use the armor of God in spiritual battles. We must pray, trust the Word, and depend on the Spirit for love, power, and grace. Then and only then will all Christians stand equipped for spiritual warfare.

APPENDIX 1

PROJECT PROPOSAL

ASHLAND THEOLOGICAL SEMINARY

EQUIPPING CHRISTIANS FOR SPIRITUAL WARFARE

A PROJECT PROPOSAL SUBMITTED TO

THE FACULTY OF ASHLAND THEOLOGICAL SEMINARY
IN PARTIAL FULFILLMENT OF THE REQUIREMENTS FOR THE
DEGREE OF DOCTOR OF MINISTRY

BY CHARLES GORDON

ASHLAND, OHIO JULY 24, 2009

EQUIPPING CHRISTIANS FOR SPIRITUAL WARFARE

The purpose of this project is to measure the impact of a six-week course at Unity Baptist Church in Detroit, Michigan on the participants' understanding of spiritual warfare as well as their identification of and use of God's armor. The research question is: What is the impact of a six-week course at Unity Baptist Church in Detroit, Michigan in equipping participants to understand spiritual warfare as well as to identify and effectively use God's armor?

The project focus is for participants to understand the nature of spiritual warfare and thereby equip them for encountering forces of darkness. The aim of the project is to introduce scriptures that are particularly meaningful to the participants in preparation for spiritual warfare.

To accomplish the purpose of the project, there will be an open invitation extended to members of Unity Baptist Church to participate in a six-week course. The participants will meet for two hours each week for six weeks at the church.

Each session will consist of time for study, prayer, and meditation. Participants will undergo Scripture selections that will focus on spiritual warfare with an emphasis on the wisdom and power of God's Word to equip believers in engaging in spiritual warfare. The class will explore concepts such as "spiritual warfare," and "equipping." Pedagogical emphasis is on theology, biblical exegesis, spiritual conflict, and the Presence of God evident in the work of the Holy Spirit. Participants will increase their understanding of spiritual warfare and be able to identify and effectively use God's armor for spiritual warfare. The outcome will be measured by a pre-and post-survey that will determine the impact of the six-week course. The pre- and post-test survey results will determine the degree to which participants are equipped in their understanding of spiritual warfare and their ability to identify and effectively use God's armor.

RATIONALE

Once one commits to following Jesus, it is a lifelong spiritual journey. The spiritual journey is often set with distracting and deceiving schemes and strategies of the evil one. His purpose is to discourage Christians. Spiritual warfare is a reality. Spiritual warfare is a daily part of a Christian's journey. There are times in my life when I desire to please the Lord and make Him proud, and yet I still encounter resistance initiated by Satan. When I am confronted by the challenges of satanic attack in life and ministry, Jesus encourages me to remain steadfast in heartfelt prayer. I have often lifted up to God my requests, desires, feelings, experiences, situations and needs. God has faithfully received my prayers and petitions. Even more, God has faithfully been my resource in times of need- particularly with my engagement in spiritual warfare.

There is a degree of courage required to be spiritually ready to be used as God's warrior. One must be vulnerable and willing to trust God to supply what is needed. In addition to prayer, God's Word brings hope, encouragement, and empowerment against the fiery darts of the devil. His Word inspires trust and is my shield against false teaching. The Word of God also directs how all Christian followers should live. Therefore, every step of our journey helps us to grow into the image of Christ and become an exemplary follower of Christ Jesus. This pleases God.

It is out of my personal experience of spiritual warfare that I have a passion to equip followers of Jesus for spiritual warfare. My personal experience informs me that many Christians underestimate the evil one's warfare against Christians. Consequently, our pews are filled with Christians who do not understand "spiritual warfare" and are not equipped to defeat Satan. For this reason, Christians are falling victim to Satan's attacks resulting in their feeling defeated, frustrated, and actually living in bondage to sin. There are many broken and wounded Christians who do not believe that spiritual warfare is a proactive approach to our faith. Many of the disciples in our churches are unlearned when it comes to the resources God has provided for us to use in encounters with the evil one.

Although I have had many spiritual warfare encounters, there is one in particular that I will never forget. It occurred in Dallas, Texas on April 4, 1999. I was at a Holiday Inn for the night, and I asked the hotel manager to give me a quiet room in the back of the hotel, Room 122, so I could pray and study the Bible. At approximately 11:30 p.m., I was awakened to a state of semi consciousness as a dark spirit being came to me and told me to get up out of the bed. A few seconds later, I saw a luminous spirit coming out of my body which said, "Let me handle this." Immediately, the dark spirit being left the room. The luminous spirit then said to me, "Rest now, but tomorrow change your room to the front." Later that week, I learned that Room 122 was used for illegal drug trafficking. The room was a stronghold for the evil one. This experience continues to be a vivid memory for me. I have a passion for equipping believers' understanding of spiritual warfare and to assist them in identifying and using God's armor.

BIBLICAL RATIONALE

Spiritual warfare is a common experience of Christians. Whether we think about it or not, the truth is that we all face supernatural opposition as we set out to live for Jesus. We have an opponent who wants nothing more than to bring about our demise. We have an enemy who wants to hinder our every effort to share the good news of liberation with those still held in captivity. Both the Old and New Testament scriptures reveal several examples of the reality of spiritual warfare and the value and importance of God's armor in preparation for battle.

The scriptures tell me this project is extremely important. Spiritual warfare is cast in scripture as an integral part of the Godly life experience. Old Testament scripture reveals in the beginning, God created the heavens and the earth. God also created man in His own image (Gen. 1:1-27) and for His glory (Isa. 43:7). "The Lord God said, 'The man has now become like one of us, knowing good and evil'" (Gen. 3:22). Although humanity was created to glorify God, respect for free will and choice allows all to accept God or to reject Him. To reject God is sin.

The first recorded instance of sin took place in Heaven. The angel Lucifer became ambitious and desired to be equal with God. For this sin of pride, he was cast out of heaven and became the one whom the Bible describes as the devil or Satan (Isa. 14:12-14). Spiritual warfare exists first in heaven. Isaiah 14:12 laments, "How you have fallen from heaven, O Morning Star, son of the dawn! You have been cast down to the earth, you who once laid low the nations." I attribute this text to be talking about Satan. A war between the forces of good and evil was under way, and this warfare was happening in heaven (Evan 1998, 30).

In the New Testament scriptures, the gospel writers penned several examples of Jesus' encounter with the devil. Jesus knew the world is full of adversarial spirits. Jesus was aware that those adversarial spirits are successful at tormenting people. Scripture teaches that Jesus was tested by Satan in the wilderness after He has fasted 40 days and nights (Matt. 4:1-11). Whenever Jesus was confronted with people filled with demons, He cast out the demons (Matt. 8:28-34). When Jesus was in the garden of Gethsemane, Satan sought to obstruct the plan of God for our salvation (Mark 14:32-41). Jesus' encounter with spiritual warfare indicates that we also should take a stand against the devil's schemes.

The Apostle Paul warned the New Testament church that we must identify and use God's armor to protect ourselves against the wiles of the devil (Arnold 2003, 30). Since the battle is not of earthly origin, we must put our faith and trust in God. We can overcome the devil's schemes with the help of the Holy Spirit (Arnold 2003, 30). Ephesians 6:17-18 affirms that the sword of the Spirit is the Word of God, which is our armor of defense and weapon of offense. Our responsibility includes also putting on the full armor of God so we, as Christians, may be able to stand victoriously (Eph. 6:11-13).

THEOLOGICAL

This project significantly rests on theological grounds because God's goal for believers is to be equipped and empowered for spiritual warfare. There are several themes that are woven through this project that reflect on many of the doctrinal items on which Christians in general adhere to and, in particular, believe.

The Holy Spirit is important to the process of spiritual warfare and change. The presence of God within the believer inspires and empowers us with qualities we would not otherwise possess. Third person in the Godhead, the Holy Spirit (Hebrew, *ruach;* Greek, *pneuma)* works within us. He blesses us. He transforms us. The Holy Spirit is our source of inspiration and power. He is the vehicle of God's revelation and activity who gives us wisdom, courage, and power to stand boldly and confidently against the devil's schemes and tricks. The Spirit makes Christians one "in Christ." God's spirit gives believers the courage to take decisive action (2 Tim. 3:15-17).

The matter of spiritual warfare is also a prominent theme throughout this project. Spiritual warfare is the invisible confrontation between the forces of God and the forces of evil, and the kingdom of God versus the kingdom of darkness. Unlike earthly warfare, spiritual warfare involves fighting an invisible enemy. Sometimes, the battle brings about circumstances that can hurt humans physically, emotionally, mentally, or spiritually (2 Kings 6: 15-18). In spiritual warfare, Satan looks for areas of weakness in our lives. He seeks ways to exploit and deceive. Spiritual warfare is the most perplexing problem ever faced by humanity (Murphy 1992, 17).

The doctrine of Satan is a prominent theme throughout this project. Scripture confirms that Satan is the foe of every human being, starting with Adam and Eve. The name "Satan" according to Harper's Bible Dictionary, 1st ed., actually means adversary or one who opposes (Achtemeier 1985). Still, many believers shy away from any discussion about spiritual warfare because they are frightened of Satan and satanic attack. But to ignore this enemy and hope he will ignore us is both unrealistic and dangerous. Therefore, the church must equip the people of God to, understand spiritual warfare, and to identify and effectively use God's armor.

HISTORICAL

Historians acknowledge that God created moral beings that obeyed His will and were able to co-exist peaceably. However, this harmony did not last. Edward Murphy said, "At some point in the hidden past, rebellion occurred within the angelic kingdom, the Kingdom of God and the Kingdom of Satan" (Murphy 1996, 13). Historians have also found references to spiritual warfare throughout the ages (Murphy 1996, 18-20).

In the 18th century, early Christian tradition indicates that spiritual warfare had its roots as far back at least to the Qumran community with its theology of cosmic conflict between good and evil. Still, it is believed that the most complex and profound dimension of spiritual warfare has to do with the origin of the conflict.

Satan and his demons came to represent the powers of evil in the universe. The hosts of Satan are committed to hinder and obstruct the work of Christ. Satan is always opposed to God's purposes for His people. In the provocative book, *The Problem of Pain,* Murphy states that C. S. Lewis practiced atheism for most of his life. In his defense of atheism, Murphy describes the evil and misfortune that plague all human beings. He concludes:

> If you ask me to believe that this is the work of a benevolent and omnipotent spirit, I reply that all the evidence points in the opposite direction. Either there is no spirit behind the universe, or else a spirit indifferent to good and evil, or else an evil spirit (Murphy 1996, 17).

The historical record tells me that this project is significant because spiritual warfare exists in our universe. Historically, the congregation at Unity Baptist Church accepts this view. Pastors and Church leaders have always addressed spiritual warfare. We believe the people of God are in a state of spiritual warfare. It is also believed that God will stand with us and fight against the schemes of the devil. The six-week small group class offered at the Unity church will be a key educational tool for equipping believers for spiritual warfare. The class could provide an opportunity for believers to understand spiritual warfare and God's available resources. I will continue the church's efforts to warn Christians that Satan fights with lies that may sound very much like the truth. The participants will be positioned to arm themselves with God's truth to defeat Satan's lies. The congregation at Unity has been taught that Satan's attacks are personal, often involving their hearts, emotions, and faith. God's righteousness can be worn as our breastplate to protect us from Satan's temptations. The church has historically provided opportunities for spiritual growth. In the war against Satan, the church must continue its efforts to equip God's people for spiritual warfare (Kraft and White 2000, 209-211).

CONTEMPORARY

There are many contemporary writers advising the church to be on guard and prepared for spiritual warfare. Drs. Charles Hodges, Joyce Meyers, Charles Stanley, Neil T. Anderson, Elizabeth Alves, and Augustus Strong have one thing in common. They are advocating the need for understanding spiritual warfare and how not to fall into the traps of the devil. According to Gregory Boyd, "...spiritual warfare affects the life of a nation, the culture in which we live" (Boyd 1997, 23). Our goals, as believers, should be to gain an accurate and sober-minded understanding of Spiritual warfare and not be led astray by a tainted view originating from frightening superstitions and odd practices. Clinton Arnold explains,

> Christians are in the midst of a struggle that is far greater than us, but it is not bigger than our God. It involves two warring kingdoms, but the sides are not at all evenly matched. There is no cosmic dualism here, with two opposing gods of near-equal power. The testimony of scripture from beginning to end is that Yahweh is sovereign. He created everything in heaven and earth. All of the spiritual powers derive their life from him. He (God) holds them in the palm of his hand, and can do with them as He will. In fact, He has already revealed the final outcome of the battle. Christians are on the winning side. (Arnold 2003, 23)

Our adversary is real. Satan is crafty, deceitful, and tricky. Satan and his host are committed to hinder and obstruct the work of Christ. The forces of evil are powerful, numerous, and organized. Charles Kraft and Mark White state:

> One of Satan's primary tactics to thwart God's plans is to get God's people to disobey him or to neglect their relationship with him. This the enemy does most effectively through either keeping people ignorant of what God desires (2 Corinthians 4:4) or by deceiving them into disobeying (Genesis 3: 1-7). (Kraft and White 2000, 47)

Pastors, preachers, and teachers warn us not to fight the devil in our own power. We must acknowledge that our personal strength is limited. Clinton Arnold said, "When Christians recognize the presence of all kinds of supernatural evil influences...God then extends 'supernatural' protection and help" (Arnold 2003, 115).

Charles Kraft argues, "For we, as Christians, have much to learn in this important area, including how to distinguish spiritual power that is from God, and spiritual power that is from the enemy" (Kraft 2002, 11). Chuck Lawless reminds us, "The enemy will do everything he can do to keep nonbelievers in his darkness, and only God is powerful enough to overcome that darkness" (Lawless 2006, 4). We must believe that strength and victory can be found only through an unwavering faith in God and using the resources God has provided.

CONTEXT

The purpose of this project is to measure the impact of a six-week course at Unity Baptist Church in Detroit, Michigan on the participants' understanding of spiritual warfare as well as their identification of and use of God's armor. Unity Baptist Church, of which I am a minister, was organized in December 1926, from a home-to-home prayer meeting. The Bible study group of eight God-fearing, African-American Christians resided on the west side of Detroit. One of the first meetings was held at the home of Mr. and Mrs. Atticus Kemp. Later, the meetings moved to the home of Reverend and Mrs. Fluker. The group quickly expanded to 18 people and they saw the need to formalize and establish a church in the community. At the suggestion of Mrs. Rosebud Smith, the name of "Unity Baptist Church" was adopted by the group. Reverend O. C. White was elected to serve as moderator.

Reverend James S. Murray was elected pastor while the group was still worshipping in the basement of the Flukers' home. He served the congregation as pastor from 1927 to 1937. In 1927, the congregation moved into its first church building, which was located at 7513 Bryden Street. The first church building was built with the assistance of its membership and friends and without the aid of a building contractor. Between 1937 and 1963, the Unity Baptist Church continued to grow. There were several pastors called and all made a difference in the lives of the parishioners and the community.

On March 17, 1963, Reverend Valmon D. Stotts was called to the pastorate of Unity Baptist Church. He began raising the congregation's awareness of his vision. Rev. Stotts' vision was for a larger and more spacious church facility in order to accommodate the rapid membership growth. Reverend Stotts also took seriously his responsibility as pastor to preach and teach the Scriptures. He encouraged all believers to follow the example of Christ and to grow to be more like Him. Reverend Stotts understood his role in the Church was a gift from God. He was chosen to perfect, equip, and build up the body of Christ so that the church would experience unity and maturity in Christ. The Apostle Paul said, "It was he who gave some to be apostles, some to be prophets, some to be evangelists, and some to be pastors and teachers, to prepare God's people for works of service, so that the body of Christ may be built up until we all reach unity in the faith and in the knowledge of the Son of God and become mature, attaining to the whole measure of the fullness of Christ..." (Eph. 4 :11-12)

Pastor Stotts established a Christian education program. The focus of this program was to connect all educational ministries in order to serve its membership and the community. The Christian education program was designed to enhance the spiritual knowledge and growth of the entire church.

The membership at Unity Baptist Church grew to approximately 3,000 in 2007. The congregation is predominantly black middle-class people. Many work as teachers, lawyers, doctors, nurses, police, preachers, and factory workers. There are also many retirees and young people. The Church has two services on Sunday morning, at 8:00 and

11:00 a.m. Since 1927 Unity Baptist Church celebrates loving God and serving God's people.

From the very beginning, Unity Baptist Church has been committed to the mandate of making disciples for Christ. Every ministry is under the guidance of the pastor and the Board of Christian Education. Equipping the people of God for service, life, and encounters with spiritual warfare continues to be a major focus of its Pastor and people. The Unity church spreads the good news of the Gospel through formal and informal educational programs. Through teaching, preaching, and caring, the church can equip its people with God's resources. The armor of God will empower them to stand effectively against the satanic attack and live victoriously.

In support of the Pastor's vision to equip the church through God's Word, a six-week course was offered to the members of Unity Baptist Church. The participants were those who were hungry for more of God and His Word. With the anointing of the Holy Spirit and the armor of God, the Unity Baptist church disciples were equipped for spiritual warfare.

SIGNIFICANT TERMS

Spiritual Warfare: The struggle between good and evil and the battle between right and wrong. Spiritual warfare refers to the believer's multidimensional war against personal sin in the battle against Satan and his fallen angels.

Eisegesis: A study process in which we read our own meaning into the passages.

Exegesis: A thorough, analytical study of a biblical passage to arrive at a useful interpretation of the passage. Exegesis is a theological task, not a mystical one.

The Armor of God: The resources God makes available to the people of God as they take up the cross and follow Christ. God's armor is a protective covering composed of truth, righteousness, peace, faith, salvation, and the sword of the Holy Spirit, which is the Word of God.

Warfare of Praise: Christian praise is offered to God during spiritual warfare, to help the believer focus on the glory of God and not on the devil. It is one of the mightiest weapons God has provided.

PROJECT GOALS

The purpose of this project is to measure the impact of a six-week course at Unity Baptist Church in Detroit, Michigan on the participants' understanding of spiritual warfare as well as their identification of and use of God's armor. The goals for this project are:

1. Participants will incorporate the concepts of the armor (weapons) of God in their faith walk.

2. Participants will gain an awareness of Satan's attacks in their lives.

3. Participants will gain an enhanced knowledge of scriptural examples that support the significance of putting on the whole armor of God.

4. Participants will deepen their awareness of the work of the Holy Spirit in victory over the forces of darkness.

5. Participants will demonstrate their understanding of spiritual warfare and God's armor.

6. Participants will practice putting on the full armor of God.

7. Participants will exercise trust in the Holy Spirit to empower them against the forces of darkness.

DēSIGN, PRōCēDURē AND ASSēSSMēNT

The research question of this project is: What is the impact of a six-week course at Unity Baptist Church in Detroit, Michigan in equipping participants to understand spiritual warfare and to identify and effectively use God's armor? The design of this project is to impact a select group of our members as they study spiritual warfare. The procedures for this project will be:

1. To determine the content and material to be taught to a group of Christians and the format in which the material will be presented;

2. To prepare a pre-test to sample the level of (a) knowledge of spiritual warfare; (b) knowledge of God's armor; and (c) knowledge of the necessity of using God's armor to effectively face spiritual darkness;

3. To administer the pre-test to the participants the first day of the six- week experience;

4. To teach the prepared material;

5. To encourage the participants to put into practice what they learned about using the full armor of God as their weapon against Satan;

6. To administer the post-test to measure the impact of the six-week group experience on each participant.

Participants of this class will learn the concepts of the full armor (weapons) of God and encouraged to stand against the devil's schemes equipped with God's resources. The group will be given the opportunity to share their experiences. The participants' thoughts, feelings, behaviors, choices, and spirituality will guide us as we review the impact of the course. The information will also guide the survey questions for the assessment of individual changes between the pre-and post-tests. Survey results will provide the data to support the content and format of the small group study and its effectiveness in equipping the participants for satanic attack. Further, it will provide strong support for the need to change.

PERSONAL GOALS

The purpose of this project is to measure the impact of a six-week small group course at Unity Baptist Church in Detroit, Michigan on the Christian individual's understanding of spiritual warfare and the identification and use of God's armor? After instructing this six-week course on spiritual warfare and the resources God has provided for combating the forces of evil, my personal goals for this project are as follows:

1. To enhance my personal knowledge of spiritual warfare and its impact on my life.

2. To gain a deeper relationship with God through Jesus Christ and the Holy Spirit.

3. To make a significant contribution to the ongoing spiritual growth of the Unity Baptist Church family, especially in areas of spiritual warfare.

4. To better prepare me to equip future believers for spiritual warfare as a result of my experience both in ministry and in preparation and the implementation of this course.

LIFE MANAGEMENT PLAN

Prepared Teaching Material .... November 2008

Pre-Survey .... January 2009

Teaching Sessions .... January 2009

Post-Survey .... January 2009

Review Survey Results .... February 2009

Submitted Project Proposal .... June 2009

Project Approval .... July 2009

Complete Literature Review .... July 2009

Evaluation of Literature .... July 2009

Evaluation Completed .... July 2009

First Draft of Final Paper .... August 2009

Final Draft of Paper .... September 2009

Oral Defense .... September 2009

Graduation .... December 2009

Cō Rē Tē AM

Academic Advisor:	Rev. Dr. Deborah Dennis Minister of Education Mt. Olivet Baptist Church Columbus, OH D. Min. Graduate of Ashland Theological Seminary
Field Consultant:	Rev. Dr. Valmon D. Stotts, Pastor Unity Baptist Church Detroit, Ml
Resource Persons:	Robert Marbry Sunday School Teacher Unity Baptist Church Detroit, Ml

                    Edmund P. Morgan
                    Associate Minister
                    Unity Baptist Church
                    Master of Ministry
                    Andersonville Theological Seminary

Field Consultant: Thomas Hamm, Pastor
                    Solid Rock Baptist Church
                    Detroit, Ml

SUPPORT TEAM

Sandra K. Gordon, wife
Tony Gordon, son
Carman Gordon, daughter
Sandra L. Gordon, daughter
Charles E. Gordon, son
Rev. Abe Kincannon, friend
Rev. Jiles Burgines, friend
Janice McNiel, friend
Elder King T. Nelson, friend
Rodney Caruthers, friend
Valerie E. Morgan, friend
Dr. Lee Solomon, friend

I will keep the support team informed of the progress of my project and seek their prayerful counsel throughout this project. I will e-mail them or phone them once a month with progress notes and prayer concerns.

WORKS CITED

Achtemeier, P. J. 1985. *Harper's Bible Dictionary* (1st ed.). San Francisco: Harper and Row.

Arnold, Clinton E. 2003. *Crucial Questions about Spiritual Warfare.* Grand Rapids, Ml: Baker Books

Betts, T. J. 2006. Surviving spiritual warfare: A life lesson from Job. *Southern Seminary Magazine,* 7-9. Volume 74.

Boyd, A. Gregory. 1997. *God at War: The Bible and Spiritual Conflict.* Downers Grove, IL: InterVarsity Press.

Easton, M.G. 1996. Easton's Bible Dictionary. Oak Harbor, WA: Logos Research Systems.

Elwell, Walter A. 2001. Tyndale Bible Dictionary. Wheaton, IL. Tyndale House Publishers.

Enns, Paul P. 1997. The Moody Handbook of Theology. Chicago, IL: Moody Press.

Erickson, J. Millard. 1998. *Christian Theology* (2nd ed.). Grand Rapids, Ml: Baker Books.

Evans, Tony. 1998. *Waging Victorious Spiritual Warfare: The Battle is the Lord's.* Chicago: Moody Press.

Kraft, H. Charles. 2002. *Confronting Powerless Christianity.* Grand Rapids, Ml: Chosen Books

Kraft, H. Charles and Mark White. 2000. *Behind Enemy Lines: An Advanced Guide to Spiritual Warfare.* Eugene, OR: Wipf and Stock Publishers.

Lawless, Chuck. 2006. But who are you? Churches that threaten the enemy. Southern *Seminary Magazine,* 2-5. Volume 74.

Murphy, Edward F. 1992. *The Handbook for Spiritual Warfare.* Nashville, TN: Thomas Nelson.

Nelson's New Illustrated Bible Dictionary. 1996. Nashville, TN: Thomas Nelson. Oropeza, B. J. 1997. *Angels, Demons & Spiritual Warfare.* Downers Grove, IL: InterVarsity Christian Fellowship.

Peterson, Eugene H. 1992. Under the Unpredictable Plant. Grand Rapids, Ml: William B. Eerdmans Publishing Company.

Plummer, Robert L. 2006. Wielding the sword of the spirit. *Southern Seminary Magazine,* 10-13. Volume 74-no. 3.

Ryrie, Charles Caldwell. 1995. A Survey of Bible Doctrine. Chicago, IL: Moody Press.

Smith, K. A. James. 2006. *Who's Afraid of Postmodernism?* Grand Rapids, Ml: Baker Books.

Wardle, Terry. 2004. *Helping Others on the Journey.* Nashville, TN: Sovereign World.

REFERENCES

Arnold, Clinton E. 2003. *Crucial Questions about Spiritual Warfare.* Grand Rapids, Ml: Baker Books.

Betts, T, J. 2006. Surviving spiritual warfare: A life lesson from Job. *Southern Seminary Magazine,* 7-9. Volume 74-no. 3.

Boyd, A. Gregory. 1997. *God at War: The Bible and Spiritual Conflict.* Downers Grove, IL: InterVarsity Press.

Cosgrove, Charles H. and Dennis D. Hatfield. 1994. *The Hidden Systems Behind The Fights: Church Conflict.* Nashville, TN: Abingdon Press.

Dickason, Fred C. 1995. *Angels: Elect & Evil.* Chicago: Moody Press. Erickson, J.

Millard. 1998. *Christian Theology* (2nd ed.). Grand Rapids, MI: Baker Books.

Evans, Tony. 1998. *Waging Victorious Spiritual Warfare: The Battle is the Lord's.* Chicago: Moody Press.

Foster, Neill K. 1995. *Warfare Weapons "Mighty Through God."* Camp Hill, PA: Horizon Books.

Hoffman, Mary T. 2006. *Spiritual Light Versus Spiritual Darkness.* Retrieved on December 5, 2006 from www.all-creatures.org/living/spirituallight.html

Kraft, H. Charles. 2002. *Confronting Powerless Christianity.* Grand Rapids, MI: Chosen Books.

Kraft, H. Charles and Mark White. 2000. *Behind Enemy Lines: An Advanced Guide to Spiritual Warfare.* Eugene, OR: Wipf and Stock Publishers.

Lawless, Chuck. 2006. But who are you? Churches that threaten the enemy. *Southern Seminary Magazine,* 2-5. Volume 74-no. 3.

Life Application Study Bible (New International Version [NIV]). 1997. Wheaton, IL: Tyndale House.

Luther, Martin. 1529. A Mighty Fortress.

Mathews, R. Arthur. 1992. *Born for Battle.* Littleton, CO: OMF Books.

Murphy, Edward F. 1992. *The Handbook for Spiritual Warfare.* Nashville, TN: Thomas Nelson.

Nelson's New Illustrated Bible Dictionary. 1996. Nashville, TN: Thomas Nelson.

Oropeza, B. J. 1997. *Angels, Demons and Spiritual Warfare.* Downers Grove, IL: InterVarsity Christian Fellowship.

Payne, Leanne. 2004. *Restoring the Christian Soul.* Grand Rapids, MI: Baker Books.

Plummer, Robert L. 2006. Wielding the sword of the spirit. *Southern Seminary Magazine,* 10-13. Volume 74-no. 3.

Richardson, Rick. 2000. *Evangelism: Outside the Box.* Downers Grove, IL: InterVarsity Press.

Seen and the Unseen Spirit. 2006. Retrieved on October 24, 2006 from www.spirithome.com/unseen.htm

Smith, K. A. James. 2006. *Who's Afraid of Postmodernism?* Grand Rapids, MI: Baker Books.

Spiritual Warfare: Know Your Enemy. 2006. Retrieved on October 24, 2006 from http://alternative-counseling.org/sp-war/sw-orig.html

Spiritual Warfare: Welcome to Let Us Reason. Retrieved on October 24, 2006 from www.letusreason.org/pent13.htmwww.en.wikipedia.org/wiki/Theological

Wagner, Peter C. 1996. *Intercessory Prayer: How God Can Use your Prayers to Move Heaven and Earth.* Ventura, CA: Regal Books.

Wardle, Terry. 2004. *Helping Others on the Journey.* Nashville.TN: Sovereign World.

Whole Armor of God. 2006. Retrieved on October 24, 2006 from www.fillthevoid.org/children/TheBattle/who-is-the-Devil/whoisthedev

APPENDIX 2

Spiritual Warfare Survey at

Unity Baptist Church, Detroit, Michigan

Pre and Post-Test Assessment

Please use the following scale to rate the effectiveness of the class, Spiritual Warfare. Circle <u>one</u> number that best represents your assessment. There are 12 statements.

> 5 = Strongly Agree
>
> 4 = Agree
>
> 3 = Neither Agree Nor Disagree
>
> 2 = Disagree
>
> 1 = Strongly Disagree

Christians believe that:

5 4 3 2 1   1. Spiritual Warfare is also defined as the invisible confrontation between the forces of God and the forces of the devil.

5 4 3 2 1   2. Scripture clearly confirms that Satan is the foe of every human being.

5 4 3 2 1   3. God's word, presented to us through Scripture, is trustworthy.

5 4 3 2 1   4. Fallen angels alert us to the way that Christians can be tempted.

5 4 3 2 1   5. Prayer is utilized as a weapon to penetrate strongholds.

5 4 3 2 1   6. Ephesians 6:11 instructs Christians to put on the full Armor of God in order to take a stand against the devil's schemes.

5 4 3 2 1	7. Spiritual Warfare is a proactive approach to the Christian faith.
5 4 3 2 1	8. Christians need divine help to deal with Satan's attacks.
5 4 3 2 1	9. The angel Lucifer became ambitious to be equal with God.
5 4 3 2 1	10. God cast Satan and his followers (1/3 of the angels) out of Heaven.
5 4 3 2 1	11. Demons are believed to be real.
5 4 3 2 1	12. God has already defeated Satan.

Comments:

_____
_____
_____
_____
_____
_____
_____
_____
_____
_____
_____
_____

WORKS CITED

Armor of God. 2007. Retrieved on December 12, 2007 from www.crossroad.to/ Victory/armor

Arnold, Clinton E. 2003. *Crucial Questions about Spiritual Warfare.* Grand Rapids, Ml: Baker Books.

Betts, T. J. 2006. Surviving spiritual warfare: A life lesson from Job. *Southern Seminary Magazine,* 7-9. Volume 74-no. 3.

Boyd, A. Gregory. 1997. *God at War: The Bible and Spiritual Conflict.* Downers Grove, IL: InterVarsity Press.

The Christian and spiritual warfare. 2006. *Southern Seminary,* 7, Volume 74-no. 3.

Dew, Diane S. 1997. *Spiritual warfare: A study in the scripture.* Retrieved On October 24, 2006 from www.dianedew.com

Dickason, Fred C. 1995. *Angels Elect & Evil.* Chicago: Moody Press.

Erickson, J. Millard. 1998. *Christian Theology* (2nd ed.). Grand Rapids, Ml: Baker Books.

Evans, Tony. 1998. *Waging victorious spiritual warfare: The battle is the Lord's.* Chicago: Moody Press.

Evil spiritual influence. 2007. Retrieved on October 16, 2007 from www.tedmontgomery .com.

Foster, Richard J. 1992. *Prayer: Finding the heart's true home.* New York: Harper Collins.

Friesen, Randy. 2006. *Equipping principles for spiritual warfare.* Retrieved on December 4, 2006 from www.search.atlaonline.com

Harper Collins Study Bible. 1985. New York: Harper Collins.

Henry, Matthew. 1961. *Matthew Henry's Commentary.* Grand Rapids, Ml:

Zondervan.

Hiebert, Paul G. 2006. *Spiritual warfare and worldviews.* Retrieved on December 4, 2006 from www.search.atlaonline.com

Holy Bible (King James version). 1983. Zondervan Corporation, Grand Rapids, Ml.

Jones, Cheslyn, Geoffrey Wainwright, and Edward Yarnold. 1986. *The Study of Spirituality.* New York: Oxford University Press.

Kaiser, Walter. 1996. *Spiritual warfare and worldviews.* Retrieved from December 4, 2006 from www. search.atlaonline.com

Kempis, Thomas A: Priest, monk, and writer. 2005. Retrieved on October 24, 2005 from www.JustUsAnglican .org

Kraft, H. Charles. 2002. *Confronting Powerless Christianity.* Grand Rapids, Ml: Chosen Books.

Kraft, H. Charles and Mark White. 2000. *Behind Enemy Lines: An Advanced Guide to Spiritual Warfare.* Eugene, OR: Wipf and Stock.

Lawless, Chuck. 2006. But who are you? Churches that threaten the enemy. *Southern Seminary Magazine,* 2-5. Volume 74-no. 3.

Let us reason. 2006. *Ministries on spiritual warfare.* Retrieved on October 24, 2006 from www.letusreason.org

Life Application Study Bible (New International Version [NIV]). 1997. Wheaton, IL: Tyndale House.

The life of Christ: Darkness and light (lesson 54). 2007. Retrieved on October 22, 2007 from www.studyjesus .com

Lovett, C. S. 1967. *Dealing with the Devil.* Baldwin Park, CA: Personal Christianity.

Mathews, R. Arthur. 1992. *Born for Battle.* OMF Books.

Murphy, Edward F. 1996. *The Handbook for Spiritual Warfare.* Nashville, TN: Thomas Nelson.

The new lie: The devil has no kingdom. 2007. Retrieved on November 3, 2007 from www.velocity.net

Oropeza, B. J. 1997. *Angels, Demons & Spiritual Warfare.* Downers Grove, IL: InterVarsity Christian Fellowship.

Payne, Leanne. 2004. *Restoring the Christian Soul.* Grand Rapids, Ml: Baker Books.

Plummer, Robert L. 2006. Wielding the sword of the spirit. *Southern Seminary Magazine,* 10-13. Volume 74-no. 3.

Sherley-Price, Leo and Kempis, Thomas A. 1996. *Imitation of Christ.* Retrieved on October 24, 2005 from www.JustUsAnglican.org

Smith, K. A. James. 2006. *Who's Afraid of Postmodernism?* Grand Rapids, Ml: Baker Books.

Spiritual warfare: Soul struggles against evil. 2007. Retrieved on November 3, 2007 from www.spirithome.com

Stedman, Ray C. 2007. *Spiritual warfare.* Retrieved on November 3, 2007 from www.raystedman.org

Theology-Wikipedia: The free encyclopedia. 2006. Retrieved on February 18, 2007 from www.en.wikipedia.org/wiki/Theological

Tolbert, John D. 2006. *Spiritual warfare: A biblical truth for warfare.* Detroit, Ml: Council of Baptist Pastors.

Vine, W. E. 1997. *Expository Dictionary of Old and New Testament Words.* Nashville, TN: Thomas Nelson.

Wardle, Terry. 2004. *Helping others on the journey.* Nashville, TN: Sovereign World.

www.directionjournal.org. 2007.

Youngblood, Ronald F. (Ed.). 1995. *Nelson's New Illustrated Bible Dictionary.* Nashville. TN: Thomas Nelson.

REFERENCES

Alves, Elizabeth. 2003. *Becoming a Prayer Warrior.* Ventura, CA: Gospel Light Publications.

Anderson, Neil. 1993. *The Bondage Breakers.* Eugene, OR: Harvest House.

Armor of God. 2007. Retrieved on February 12, 2007 from www.crossroad.to/Victory/armor

Arnold, Clinton E. 2003. *Crucial questions about spiritual warfare.* Grand Rapids, Ml: Baker Books.

Arnold, Clinton E. 1989. Ephesians Power and Magic, Grand Rapids, Ml Baker Books.

Arthur, Kay. 1991. *Lord, is it warfare? Teach me to stand.* Sisters, OR: Multnomah Books.

Betts, T. J. 2006. Surviving spiritual warfare: A life lesson from Job. *Southern Seminary,* 7-9. Volume 74-no. 3.

Boyd, A. Gregory. 1997. *God at War: The Bible and Spiritual Conflict.* Downers Grove, IL: InterVarsity Press.

The Christian and spiritual warfare. 2006. *Southern Seminary,* 7, Volume 74-no. 3.

Cosgrove, Charles H. and Dennis D. Hatfield. 1994. *The Hidden Systems Behind the Fights: Church Conflict.* Nashville, TN: Abingdon Press.

Dew, Diane S. 1997. *Spiritual warfare: A study in the scripture.* Retrieved on October 24, 2006 from www.dianedew.com

Dickason, Fred C. 1995. *Angels elect & evil.* Chicago: Moody Press.

Erickson, J. Millard. 1998. *Christian theology* (2nd ed.). Grand Rapids, Ml: Baker Books.

Evans, Tony. 1998. *Waging victorious spiritual warfare: The battle is the Lord's*. Chicago: The Moody Bible Institute.

Evans, William. 1974. *The great doctrines of the Bible*. Chicago: The Moody Bible Institute.

Foster, Neill K. 1995. *Warfare weapons "Mighty through God."* Camp-Hill, PA: Horizon Books.

Foster, Richard J. 1992. *Prayer: Finding the Heart's True Home*. New York: Harper Collins.

Friesen, Randy. 2006. *Equipping principles for spiritual warfare*. Retrieved on December 4, 2006 from www.search.atlaonline.com

Harper Collins Study Bible. 1985. New York: Harper Collins.

Henry, Matthew. 1961. *Matthew Henry's Commentary*. Grand Rapids, Ml: Zondervan.

Hiebert, Paul G. 2006. *Spiritual warfare and worldviews*. Retrieved on December 4, 2006 from www.search.atlaonline.com

Hodge, Charles. 2008. *Systematic Theology*. Charleston, SC: Bibliolife Publishers.

Hoffman, Mary T. 2006. *Spiritual light versus spiritual darkness*. Retrieved on December 5, 2006 from www.all-creatures.org/living/ spirituallight.html

Holy Bible (King James version). 1983. Zondervan Corporation, Grand Rapids, Ml.

Jones, Cheslyn, Geoffrey Wainwright, and Edward Yarnold. 1986. *The Study of Spirituality*. New York: Oxford University Press.

Kaiser, Walter. 1996. *Spiritual warfare and worldviews*. Retrieved from December 4, 2006 from www.search.atlaonline .com

Kempis, Thomas A: Priest, monk, and writer. 2005. Retrieved on October 24, 2005 from www.JustUsAnglican.org

Kraft, H. Charles. 2002. *Confronting Powerless Christianity.* Grand Rapids, Ml: Chosen Books.

Kraft, H. Charles and Mark White. 2000. *Behind enemy lines: An advanced guide to spiritual warfare.* Eugene, OR: Wipf and Stock.

Lawless, Chuck. 2006. But who are you? Churches that threaten the enemy. *Southern Seminary Magazine,* 2-5. Volume 74-no. 3.

Let us reason. 2006. *Ministries on spiritual warfare.* Retrieved on October 24, 2006 from www.letusreason.org

Life Application Study Bible (New International Version [NIV]). 1997. Wheaton, IL: Tyndale House.

The Life of Christ: Darkness and light (Lesson 54). 2007. Retrieved on October 22, 2007 from www.studyjesus.com

Lovett, C. S. 1967. *Dealing with the devil.* Baldwin Park, CA: Personal Christianity.

Mathews, R. Arthur. 1992. *Born for Battle.* OMF Books.

Murphy, Edward F. 1996. *The Handbook for Spiritual Warfare.* Nashville, TN: Thomas Nelson.

Meyers, Joyce. 2002. *Battlefield of the Mind: Winning the Battle in your Mind.* New York: Warner.

The New lie: The devil has no kingdom. 2007. Retrieved on November 3, 2007 from www.velocity.net

Oropeza, B. J. 1997. *Angels, Demons & Spiritual Warfare.* Downers Grove, IL: InterVarsity Christian Fellowship.

Payne, Leanne. 2004. *Restoring the Christian soul.* Grand Rapids, Ml: Baker Books.

Plummer, Robert L. 2006. Wielding the sword of the spirit. *Southern Seminary,* 10-13. Volume 74-no. 3.

Richardson, Rick. 2000. *Evangelism: Outside the box.* Downers Grove, IL: InterVarsity Press.

Seen and the unseen spirit. 2006. Retrieved on October 24, 2006 from www.spirithome.com/unseen.htm

Sherley-Price, Leo and Kempis, Thomas A. 1996. *Imitation of Christ.* Retrieved on October 24, 2005 from www.JustUsAnglican.org

Smith, K. A. James. 2006. *Who's afraid of postmodernism?* Grand Rapids, Ml: Baker Books.

Spiritual warfare: Know your enemy. 2006. Retrieved on October 24, 2006 from http://alternative-counseling.org/sp-war/sw-orig.html

Spiritual warfare: Soul struggles against evil. 2007. Retrieved on November 3, 2007 from www.spirithome.com

Spiritual warfare: Wikipedia. Retrieved on October 24, 2006 from http://en.wikipedia.org

Stanley, Charles. 2004. *When the Enemy Strikes.* Nashville, TN: Thomas Nelson Publishers.

Stedman, Ray C. 2007. *Spiritual warfare.* Retrieved on November 3, 2007 from www.raystedman.org

Strong, Augustus H. 2009. *Systematic Theology.* Charleston, SC: Bibliobazaar Publishers.

Tolbert, John D. 2006. *Spiritual warfare: A biblical truth for warfare.* Detroit, Ml: Council of Baptist Pastors.

Theology-Wikipedia: The free encyclopedia. 2006. Retrieved on February 18, 2007 from www.en.wikipedia.org/wiki/Theological

Vine, W. E. 1997. *Expository dictionary of old and new testament words.* Nashville, TN: Thomas Nelson.

·Wagner, Peter C. 1996. *Intercessory Prayer: How God Can Use Your Prayers to Move Heaven and Earth.* Ventura, CA: Regal Books.

Wardle, Terry. 2004. *Helping others on the journey.* Nashville, TN: Sovereign World.

Water, Mark. 2002. *World religions.* Chattanooga, TN: John Hunt Publishers.

Whole armor of God. 2006. Retrieved on October 24, 2006 from www.fillthevoid.org/children/

Wood, D.R. W. 1996. The *New Bible Dictionary.* InterVarsity Press.

The Battle/who-is-the-Devil/html. www.directionjournal.org. 2007.

Youngblood, Ronald F. (Ed.). 1995. *Nelson's New Illustrated Bible Dictionary.* Nashville. TN: Thomas Nelson.

ABOUT THE AUTHOR

Charles Gordon, Sr. is a man whose personal struggles and challenges with Satan have made him cry out to the Lord. As an overcomer of Satanic schemes such as loneliness, disappointment and discouragement, the Lord has chosen, called, anointed, and equipped him with a passion to equip Christians for spiritual warfare. As a minister of the gospel, his desire to equip Christians compelled him to pursue a Doctorate Degree in Theology. In 2009, Dr. Gordon graduated from Ashland Theological Seminary thoroughly equipped both experientially and academically to empower Christians who do not understand "spiritual warfare" so that they will no longer underestimate the evil one's warfare against them.

As a husband, father, and grandfather Dr. Gordon has experienced the joys and sorrows of life. Despite the loss of his daughter, Nakia, by suicide in 1998 and the illness and subsequent death of his beloved wife of 42 years, Rev. Sandra K. Gordon, in 2014, the faith of Dr. Charles Gordon remains as a testament to his remaining children, grandchildren and all believers that the Holy Spirit provides courage, peace, hope, and stability to those who *know* Jesus Christ, and are equipped to fight the good fight of faith!

To contact Rev. Gordon for seminars and workshops:

Rev. Dr. Charles Gordon, Sr.
c/o PriorityONE Publications
P.O. Box 34722
Detroit, MI 48234

info@RevCharlesGordon.com
www.RevCharlesGordon.com

www.ingramcontent.com/pod-product-compliance
Lightning Source LLC
Chambersburg PA
CBHW070110120526
44588CB00032B/1409